Daily We Touch Him
Practical Religious Experiences

D0188293

Daily We Touch Him
Practical Religious Experiences

M. Basil Pennington,o.c.s.o.

A SHEED & WARD BOOK

ROWMAN & LITTLEFIELD PUBLISHERS, INC.
Lanham • Boulder • New York • Toronto • Plymouth, UK

Grateful acknowledgment is given for copyright reprint permissions as
follows:

Excerpts from *The New Man* by Thomas Merton. Copyright © 1961 by
The Abbey of Gethsemani. Copyright renewed © 1989 by The Trustees
of the Merton Legacy Trust. Reprinted by permission of Farrar, Straus &
Giroux, Inc.

Excerpt from *No Man Is an Island* by Thomas Merton, copyright © 1955
by The Abbey of Our Lady of Gethsemani and renewed 1983 by the
Trustees of the Merton Legacy Trust, reprinted by permission of
Harcourt Brace & Company.

Excerpts from *A Testament of Devotion* by Thomas R. Kelly, copyright ©
1941 by Harper & Row, Publishers, Inc. Reprinted by permission of
HarperCollins Publishers.

Excerpts from *What Are These Wounds?* by Thomas Merton reprinted by
permission of Thomas Merton Legacy Trust.

Excerpts from *Zen and the Birds of Appetite*, by Thomas Merton.
Copyright ©1968 by The Abbey of Gethsemani, Inc. Excerpts from *New
Seeds of Contemplation*, by Thomas Merton. Copyright ©1961 by The
Abbey of Gethsemani, Inc. Reprinted by permission of New Directions
Publishing Corp.

Excerpts from *Prayer: Conversing With God* by Rosalind Rinker.
Copyright © 1970 by Zondervan Publishing House. Used by permission
of Zondervan Publishing House.

Excerpts from *Prayer* by Abhishiktananda (Henri Le Saux, O.S.B.).
Copyright © 1967 by Abhishiktananda. Permission in process.

Copyright© 1997 by M. Basil Pennington, o.c.s.o.

Library of Congress Cataloguing-in-Publication Data pending.
Pennington, M. Basil.
    Daily we touch Him : practical religious experiences / M. Basil
Pennington.
        p.   cm.
    Includes bibliographical references
    ISBN: 1-55612-980-7 (alk. paper)
    1. Prayer—Christianity. 2. Meditation—Christianity. 3. Spiritual life
—Christianity. I. Title.
BV210.2.P44 1997
243.3—dc21   97-6104
                                                                CIP

A SHEED & WARD BOOK
ROWMAN & LITTLEFIELD PUBLISHERS, INC.
Published in the United States of America
by Rowman & Littlefield Publishers, Inc.
A wholly owned subsidiary of The Rowman & Littlefield Publishing Group, Inc.
4501 Forbes Boulevard, Suite 200, Lanham, Maryland 20706
www.rowmanlittlefield.com

Contents

ACKNOWLEDGMENTS v

WELCOME vi

FOREWORD xiii

ONE   Faith Building: Sacred Reading 1

TWO   Faith Experiencing: Centering Prayer
• Prayer of Quiet 20

THREE   Centering Prayer: Merton •
Abhishiktananda • Van Kaam 50

FOUR   Centering Prayer and TM 61

FIVE   TM and Christian Prayer 66

SIX   Prayer and Liberation 76

SEVEN   Faith Sharing 88

EIGHT   Mary: The Faith-full Woman 102

EPILOGUE   A Rule of Life 113

BIBLIOGRAPHY 120

To Two Mothers

The Glorious Queen of Heaven
through whom all good things come

And That Wonderful Woman
who imaged her love for me on earth.

Acknowledgments

I WISH TO EXPRESS MY GRATITUDE TO MY COMMUNITY and abbot who not only enabled me to prepare this book but who are the channel through whom I received the heritage it shares. Especially am I indebted to my confrere, Father William Meninger, who provided much of the initial inspiration and incentive in precising these methods. The major religious superiors by their invitation to serve on the Religious Life Committee and their very open sharing in the workshops helped to bring this presentation of age-old methods to greater clarity. For this and so much more I say to each one of them, thank you. And I would add a very special word of thanks to that wonderful old nun, Sister M. De Sales, who, after her hours of prayer for me and my work, sits down at her typewriter and transforms my pages of scratch into beautiful manuscript. The Lord Himself is her reward. She wants no other. And so may it be for us all.

Welcome

IT HAS BEEN OVER TWENTY YEARS SINCE THIS BOOK first saw the light of day. It is a book that was in fact never really written. John Delaney, that forward-looking editor who always had his ear to the ground, approached me in the fall of 1975, asking if I had written anything on Centering Prayer. I had been teaching it for a few years then. At the moment when he called me I was about to leave the United States for the monastic republic of Mount Athos for six months of deeper solitude. I told John I had only transcripts of the talks which I had been giving at workshops. He made a proposal: He would turn the tapes into a book if I would agree to give him the journal from my Mount Athos sojourn. Good to his word, when I arrived back in New York the following spring John presented me with the first copy of *Daily We Touch Him* and then proceeded to turn my journal into a book called *O Holy Mountain*. Thus you will find the pages of this book, if not particularly polished, certainly very actual words that passed straight from my heart and mouth into the ears of my listeners.

In 1971 when Pope Paul VI asked us Cistercians to help the Church re-find its contemplative dimension, we felt quite challenged. The only method of prayer that was truly widespread among our Catholic people was the rosary. It was the only method of prayer that was taught in a simple, direct way, so that the beginner could immediately go home and start practicing it. Certainly the rosary can lead one into contemplative prayer; there is no doubt about it. I saw this in my mother and my grandmother. But this was usually only after years of practice, in the years of one's retirement, when one had the leisure to sit quietly for hours and enter deeply into the mysteries of the decades. Our challenge was to find a way to share the more contemplative methods of our ancient Christian tradition in a similarly simple and practical way.

We had what has been called our Benedictine method (though it certainly belongs to the whole Christian community): *lectio divina.* This method begins with wisely listening to what God has to say to us through his sacred Scriptures, receiving from him a "word of life" that we can carry with us through the day, letting that word form our mind and heart, coloring all that we do, making it all prayer. In apt moments, it leads to just sitting quietly with the Lord, resting with him, and accepting his invitation: Come to me all you who work hard and are heavily burdened and I will refresh you. As we continue to quietly listen to the Lord, *lectio* more and more frequently leads us into *contemplatio,* that quiet sitting with the Lord in the restfulness of love.

In the frenetic climate of our world, such leisure, such ample space and quiet are not easy to come by. This situation is not something peculiar to our twentieth century. It was ever thus in the world of human striving. It was way back in the fourth century that a young man by the name of John Cassian went in search of a solution to this. His search brought him to the fabled Abba Isaac, reputedly the holiest, oldest, and wisest father of the desert. From this master John learned what we call today Centering Prayer. When he returned to his native France, he wrote down all that Abba Isaac had taught him. Thus we have the earliest Latin description of this way of prayer. Of course it had already been written about by the Greek Fathers. They called it *monologion,* the "one-word" prayer.

Benedict of Nursia, when he wrote his *Rule for Monasteries,* sent his sons and daughters to John Cassian for their deeper instruction on prayer. The practice was passed on through the centuries in the monasteries and out among the people. When most of the monasteries in western Europe were destroyed by the Reformation and French Revolution, the practice was largely lost in the west. The challenge for us monks in the latter days of this twentieth century was to share again this tradition and to do it in a very simple way that anyone could easily learn and practice in daily life.

We began to undertake this in the little retreat house at Saint Joseph's Abbey, Spencer, Massachusetts. As we began, we certainly had no expectation that we were inaugurating what would become a worldwide movement. After we had been teaching the Prayer (it had not yet received the modern American name of "Centering Prayer") for some months, I was invited by the Conference of Major Superiors of Men to be part of their Spiritual Life Committee. This committee joined forces with the corresponding committee of the Leadership Conference of Religious Women. Soon Centering Prayer was being practiced in all parts of the United States. *Daily We Touch Him* then appeared and played its role in this outreach. As the book was translated into other languages, it contributed to bringing the prayer to other parts of the Christian world.

While the "three rules" for *lectio divina* (Sacred Reading) have remained quite stable, the "three rules" for Centering Prayer, which you will find in this volume, have been slightly refined over the course of our years of teaching. The formula we have settled upon is this. As you sit relaxed and quiet:

1. Be in faith and love to God who dwells in the center of your being.

2. Take up a love word and let it be gently present, supporting your being to God in faith-filled love.

3. Whenever you become aware of anything, simply, gently return to God with the use of your prayer word.

At the end, let the Our Father silently pray itself within you.

In more recent years Abbot Thomas Keating has presented the method in a more psychological way, reaching out to a wider audience beyond the Christian community. These are the guidelines he is presently using:

1. Choose a sacred word as the symbol of your intention to consent to God's presence and action within.

2. Sitting comfortably and with eyes closed, settle briefly and silently introduce the sacred word as the symbol of your consent to God's presence and God's action within.

3. When you become aware of thoughts, return ever so gently to the sacred word.

4. At the end of the prayer period, remain in silence with eyes closed for a couple of minutes.

Father notes that "'thoughts' [as he uses the word in his guidelines] is an umbrella term for every perception including sense perceptions, feelings, images, memories, reflections, and commentaries." As you can readily see, this is the same traditional method offered again in a simple, easily learned formula.

The spiritual masters of all traditions insist, and we totally agree with them, that fidelity to practice is the important thing. Twice a day for twenty minutes is a formula that works for most people, though there certainly is freedom to increase the time or number of meditations. Transformation of consciousness through higher levels of consciousness (or, as we realize in our Christian theology, through the increased activity of the gifts of Holy Spirit) does not ordinarily take place the first time we meditate nor the fiftieth but is a gradual process of liberation from the false self.

What is also very evident from the experience of these past twenty years is that it is a rare person who is able to be faithful to practice without some support, be it from family, community, prayer group, or the like. To this end, as well as to train teachers to foster the availability of this tradition, there has come into being an international lay organization called Contemplative Outreach. The Outreach, which is most active in the United States, the Philippines, and South Africa, has a regular newsletter, distributes tapes and books, and offers programs of many kinds. There is also a special interreligious program, called the Mastery Foundation, which enables those whose lives are about sacred ministry to empower their ministry through Centering Prayer. The Mastery Foundation has been able to bring Protestant and Catholic clergy together in such troubled areas as Northern Ireland and Central Africa as well as many other places.

Today Centering Prayer is practiced in all parts of the world – I myself have taught it on five continents – and by members of many different religions, practitioners adapting their understanding of it in line with their own particular religious beliefs. I could relate innumerable fascinating stories, but that is the matter for another book.

After hundreds of thousands of copies of this book had been distributed and several other books on Centering Prayer had been published, the original publisher allowed *Daily We Touch Him* to go out of print. But requests for this little book have never ceased to come in. I am very grateful to Robert Heyer, the Editor-in-Chief of Sheed & Ward for the opportunity to make it available again. We can humbly hope it will continue to serve the Christian community as that community reclaims its contemplative heritage.

Even after twenty years of teaching I still find many Christians who are surprised to learn that we do have a "Christian meditation," that we do not have to go to the Hindus or Buddhists if we want to learn to meditate. I look forward to the day when every Christian parish has a meditation group and makes this practical teaching readily available to all the members of the parish, and to the time when Christian meditation centers will be as present to our society as are the meditation centers of other traditions.

We live in a very frenetic world. And frankly I do not know how anyone can hope to survive and survive well without meditation. Peaceful sleep does relieve us of some of the tensions that invade us each day. Routine exercise is also helpful in this respect. But everyone who has studied the matter agrees that meditation is the best and most effective way to rid ourselves of tension and its deadly effects on our minds and bodies. Our divine Master, who said he came to seek not the well but the sick (he was speaking of spiritual health and sickness in this instance), extends to each one of us his gracious invitation: "Come to me all you who work hard and are heavily burdened, and I will refresh you." We go to Centering Prayer first of all to seek the Master himself, to give him ourselves, and to give him our love. But we seek also that refreshment, the wholeness and healing which he invites us to find with him. And where do we find him? We find him within, at the center of our being where he constantly brings us forth in his creative love. It is there that daily we want to touch him.

Father M. Basil, o.c.s.o.

Foreword

THE SUBTITLE OF THIS LITTLE BOOK IS *PRACTICAL Religious Experiences.* I hope no one for that reason thinks it is exclusively or even primarily intended for those among the People of God whom we are accustomed to refer as "religious." Certainly I do hope it will be useful for them, too, but what I have to share here I want to share with all my fellow Christians and any person who is a true seeker.

This book was originally entitled "Practical Spiritual Experiences." But that brings to mind an expression which I hate with a holy hatred: "the spiritual life." We are not *spirits*. We are very much incarnate, men and women of flesh and blood. Anyone who thinks he is a spirit, or has a spiritual life, has a lot yet to learn. It is the whole of us that was made to find delight in the Lord, not just our "spirit."

But there is another reason why I hate this expression, "spiritual life." What is a "spirit"? At best, a rather vague sort of thing. Who can get a hand on it?

One of the results of this kind of terminology and the thinking that goes with it is that when it comes to our "spiritual life" – what is indeed our *real* life – we, who are eminently practical people – people who can get a man on the moon and build billion-dollar businesses – become utterly impractical. What can you do about a spirit? And so in practice, when it comes to our "spiritual life," our life in the Spirit, we just sort of wait for something to happen. And as a result, nothing much does happen. Thus a very important dimension of our being as human persons does not develop. This leads to a lot of poorly grounded activity, activism, emptying (in the wrong sense), and ultimately frustration, boredom, meaninglessness. We need to be *very practical* about our real life and every dimension of it.

On the other hand, I like the expression "religious life." The word "religious" comes from the Latin *religare*, to be bound up again. What we do indeed want is to be "bound up" with God, to be intimately in union and communion with Him, daily to touch Him. But we have all gone away from God, beginning with our father Adam, who hid in the bushes. We share in his alienation, whether we like it or not, and that of our whole race. And we have added to it our own. "He who says he has no sin in him is a liar." The whole quest of our lives is a return, to be bound again to God. Actually it has been already accomplished. Christ Jesus, God's very Son, God Himself, one with the Father in the Love who is the Holy Spirit, has incorporated us (in a very literal sense) into Himself and given us His Spirit. This is the reality. And we need to be in touch with – daily to touch – God, to experience God, to experience our own "Godness." We need to appropriate in an experimental way by living faith – experience what is already ours through Baptism.

Touch is the most basic sense in man – the first to come, the last to leave – and it is all-pervasive. God is present to us from the very first instant that He calls us into being – and thenceforth forever! He touches us at every point and level of being. God is present to us. But are we present to Him? Daily – and many times a day – we need to touch Him, we need to experience His all-presence and be present to our true selves in Him. The air is all about us, touching us at every point of our body – but how much of the time are we unconscious of its touch. So it is with God. When Christ told us to pray without ceasing, He was calling us to come into awareness of what is, to be present to His constant, all-pervasive communication of Himself to us. The first step toward fulfilling this evangelical command is to be sure that at least at some moments in each day's passing we are present; it is to learn practically how to come into presence and to program times for this in our oftentimes too busy lives.

In this book we offer a few practical exercises to help us do this. In themselves they ask little of us. Perhaps the greatest asceticism they ask is making room for them, letting go of a lot of less fruitful, even inconsequential, things. But simple though these practices are, they can and they will, if pursued with some fidelity, profoundly change and enrich our lives.

I say this with the testimony of experience. I can speak from my own life experience, but also from those of many others. These practices, as they are spelled out here, come directly from the practical religious experience workshops that I, along with others, have been conducting the past few years, first for the major religious superiors of the United States, then for priests and most recently for lay adults and students. Over the course of the years I have been able to see the fruit of these practices in the lives of these men and women. Some of the groups who have made the workshops have spontaneously decided to continue to meet periodically to share their growing experience. Others I have met only at random. Yet again and again, often with great enthusiasm, these men and women have witnessed to the great changes that have come about in their lives since they began to make a place in their day for these exercises. Their experience can be summed up as a maturing of those qualities of life that Saint Paul speaks of as the fruits of the Spirit: love, joy, peace, patience, kindness, goodness, trustfulness, gentleness and self-control (Gal. 5:22-23). Who does not want these to be deeply and pervasively present in his or her life?

One of the things that I have tried constantly to insist upon in the workshops is that we be not only receivers but givers. "Freely have you received, freely give." Those who have made these workshops have gone on to share these practices with others. They are so simple that anyone can learn them readily and then go on to teach them. And that is what I hope each reader will do. Too long have we left all the ministry in our Church to priests and religious. Every Christian has been baptized into the priesthood of Christ. This means that all have a call, a "vocation," to minister to all their fellows. The readiness to share these practices bears witness not only to the fact that they are valued and considered worth sharing but also that they are actually enlivening the basic Christian vocation, that they are allowing the Spirit of Christ to function more fully in the lives of the sharers.

I must confess, though, that it has been with some hesitation and only after a good bit of prodding from those who have made the workshops, as well as some serious searching in prayer, that I have undertaken to attempt to share these things in writing. Christian life is life, and it is most properly engendered by one who has attained a certain maturity in it, a certain fullness, and engendered in another in a very personal way. The tradition of the spiritual father and spiritual mother has been very strong wherever Christian life has been most vital. Other traditions, too, have stressed the importance of the immediate guidance of the spiritual master, the roshi, the guru. The writings that have come down to us describing the deeper ways of prayer, such as those on the Jesus Prayer, or *The Cloud of Unknowing*, seem to presuppose a personal teaching. The reader rarely draws out of the writings themselves the essential method or way of prayer they describe, often in rich analogy. To attempt to hand on these practices by means of a book rather than by personal sharing in a context of prayer and presence somewhat frightens me. I fear the reader will receive something, feel he or she has the essence, attempt the practice, and perhaps have a very frustrating experience, and then close the door on what should have been for him or her an avenue to fuller life and love. For this reason I would indeed exhort the reader to approach these chapters prayerfully, earnestly seeking the presence and enlightening help of the Holy Spirit. Saint Paul writes to the Corinthians:

> The hidden wisdom of God which we teach in our mysteries is the wisdom God predestined to be for our glory before the ages began. It is a

wisdom that none of the masters of this age have ever known . . . We teach what Scripture calls: the things that no eye has seen and no ear has heard, things beyond the mind of man, all that God has prepared for those who love Him.

These are the very things that God has revealed to us through the Spirit, for the Spirit reaches the depths of everything, even the depths of God. After all, the depths of a man can only be known by his own spirit, not by any other man, and in the same way the depths of God can only be known by the Spirit of God. Now instead of the spirit of the world, we have received the Spirit that comes from God, to teach us to understand the gifts that He has given us. Therefore we teach, not in the way in which philosophy is taught, but in the way that the Spirit teaches us; we teach spiritual things spiritually. An unspiritual person (one who does not have the Holy Spirit) is one who does not accept anything of the Spirit of God. He sees it all as nonsense, it is beyond his understanding because it can only be understood by means of the Spirit. A spiritual man, on the other hand, is able to judge the value of everything . . . (1 Cor. 2:7-15)

May the Holy Spirit be with you as you journey through this book and through life. It is a journey of faith – faith building, faith experiencing, faith sharing – until faith gives way to vision, and life is not ended, but changed, and we share together the vision. Father, let it be so!

Fr. M. Basil, o.c.s.o.

ONE

Faith Building

Sacred Reading
"The just man lives by faith."

IT IS IMPOSSIBLE TO EXAGGERATE THE FUNDAMENTAL role of faith in Christian life. Indeed, without faith there is no Christian life, for I can truly love Christ and follow Him only insofar as I know Him by faith. Prayer, a loving response to and communion with God, must start from faith, for hope and love are but faith moving toward its Object.

Faith is simply: I believe, it is so, I am certain of it, because He has said it. It involves two elements: knowing Him and knowing what He has said. This affirmation, this certitude, is basically possible only because He has given me the gift we call faith – a divinizing power of the intellect, moved by the will, to accept without doubt what He says, because He says it. Given this basic power, the use of it grows as my knowledge of Him and of what He has taught grows. Above all, what He teaches, what He reveals is Himself, and His love for me, which is Himself.

Faith is the foundation of my life as a Christian. The day in which I do not grow in faith, I do not truly grow. How, then, do I grow in faith?

If "faith comes through hearing," I grow in faith through hearing. Each day I want to meet with Him that I might hear Him.

"HE STILL PROCLAIMS HIS GOSPEL"

The primary place Christ speaks to His people and feeds their faith is in the proclamation of the Gospel in the midst of the Church assembled.

"In the Liturgy God speaks to His people and Christ is still proclaiming His Gospel" (Constitution on the Sacred Liturgy, 33).

There is power in the Word and a special power in this moment of solemn proclamation. If I have ears and am truly listening, I will receive this Word and it will come alive in my heart.

But as powerful as this moment is, in practice, it is not always the most fruitful. For one reason, the liturgical celebration moves right on. It is a community thing.

The priest, as the leader, is at a special disadvantage, as he must at this time be concerned with ministry and cannot turn his whole attention to humbly receiving the Word and letting it come alive in him. He should, though, prepare well and be concerned that he so leads the celebration of the Liturgy of the Word that the hearers, the community assembled, can have the best possible presentation and context in which to receive the Word. The community is, to some extent, at his mercy, and those who assist him. How he helps the community to prepare to receive the Word through penitence and prayer, how the actual texts are proclaimed, to what extent the community is given spaces for silence to let the Word germinate and come to life within, how significant elements are underlined in the homily will greatly affect the fruitful reception of the Word by each member of the community.

Even when all these elements are at their best, the recipient still has problems. The service must move along. There can only be a very limited time, at best, to savor, share, respond. Moreover, Mother Church is a loving, indulgent mother. She always sets before us a rich banquet. I can hardly hope to digest all the richness of each day's readings, especially on Sundays and Feasts when an extra reading is added. It is too much. And in trying to get all, I may end up getting nothing. Who has not had the experience at times of discovering at the end of the Liturgy that, though he was attentive in general, he cannot recall exactly what the readings of the day had to say?

Here I would like to make one very simple suggestion. It is a practice I have found personally fruitful. Instead of trying to devour the whole content of all the readings, try to single out just one particular morsel, hold on to it, chew it, perhaps return to it in the pause after Communion and talk to Christ about it. And then carry it through the day. If at each Liturgy I can let one Word come alive in me, in time I will be exceedingly enriched.

SACRED FAITH

Another choice moment for hearing the Word and growing in faith is when Christians come together. "Where two or three are gathered in my name, there am I in the midst of them." Christ is present, and we are to speak the Word of faith to one another in His name. The living faith I have within me is His gracious gift and I am meant to share it with others. "Freely have you received, freely give." As I speak the Word, my brother or sister hears, and faith grows in the hearer, who in turn speaks the life-giving Word to me.

In this, I fear many of us have to admit we have been very shy. We sometimes seem to be able to talk freely, at length, and with joy and enthusiasm about almost anything except that which is most fundamental: Jesus Christ and His activity in our lives. Sometimes we feel it is almost indecent to reveal such deeply intimate things, or it might be boastful, or give others the wrong idea about us. This is true even in religious communities, and among priests who regularly proclaim the faith to others in the course of their ministry. I might even say it is often more true of these. Yet have not religious come together precisely to form communities of faith and to help each other grow in faith?

I have found that when I have the courage to speak out and share, the response has always been a very positive one. And soon my brother is sharing with me some of the wonderful things the Lord of Faith is doing in his own life or some of his struggles in faith. It becomes a very rich and enriching sharing. But someone needs to have the courage to initiate the sharing, to open the door to these deeper, more sacred regions of our being and living.

SACRED READING

If it is true that the Word-bearing faith does come to me primarily at the liturgical assembly and in faith sharing, it is yet true that in both of these there are circumstances beyond my control. I must move along with the rest at the Liturgy and I can share with others only to the extent they are willing, given my initiation, to allow this to happen. But there is one situation where I do have considerable autonomy and control, and that is in the hearing of the printed word, in sacred reading. Here I am free to take up the text when and where I will, to move along at my own pace, to take all the time I want to savor the Word, to let it resound within me and to respond to it – indeed, to fight it, if I will, or to receive it with docility, and let it soothe and fill a hungry spirit.

In talking about faith-building reading I like to distinguish four kinds of sacred reading, although in practice they do at times all come together in the same experience.

A. Sacred Study

We are living in one of the most privileged times in the history of the human race. Not only is it a post-conciliar period (and there have been only twenty of them through the twenty centuries of Christianity), but we are living at the time of a new Pentecost. In response to the humble prayer of His Vicar, Christ the Lord has sent forth the Holy Spirit in a new and powerful way to enliven the Church and the whole human family. As Christ promised at the meal of love He shared with His friends the night before He ascended to the Cross, He has sent the Spirit, the Paraclete, to strengthen and to console, and to teach us all things – to help us to enter into the deep mysteries of God and of Christ's mission of love.

We are all used to the idea of the development of dogma – no new Revelation but a deepening under-

standing of it, a more apt expression of it – more apt
for our times. The Holy Spirit is powerfully at work
in the Church today, and this development is
moving ahead rapidly. In practice, I cannot expect
the Holy Spirit to work in my own life, nor in the life
of anyone I am sharing with, through yesterday's
theology. He is leading us along to minister to our
needs today. And so it is incumbent upon me to keep
abreast, to do sacred study regularly to hear what
the Spirit is saying to the Churches today.

If this is true of every Christian, it is preeminently
true of the professionals – priests and religious. No
one wants to depend on the service of one who is
outdated. Who would go to a doctor if he knew the
doctor was still depending wholly on what he
learned in medical school ten or fifteen years ago –
or even just last year? We want our man to have the
latest and the best.

Priests and religious can look to professionals in
other fields for examples here. I can think of a case in
my own family. A few years ago one of my relatives
was hospitalized. The cause of his condition was
obscure. His own doctor tried various things. The
months wore on. Then one day another relative, who
happens to be a doctor, went to visit the sick man. This
doctor's specialty was in a very different area. Yet he
constantly made an effort to keep up with all the
developments in the field of medicine. He perused the
important journals, shared in a digest service, listened
to cassettes as he drove around. His expert eye quickly
sized up his uncle's situation. He checked the history
of the case and then recommended a new drug. Within
a few days the sufferer was out of the hospital and on

his way back to work. His own doctor was a good man, but he was not keeping up.

Earlier this year I had the misfortune of being involved in a legal case in a distant city. On advice, those whom I was associated with hired a local lawyer. The case seemed quite clear, the injustice of our adversary quite evident. But when we appeared in court, his lawyer cited a recent amendment to the city's statutory law. Our lawyer was not familiar with it and could not respond. We lost the case and had to renegotiate. Needless to say, we were happy to be relieved of that lawyer's "service."

The ministry of law is important; the ministry of medicine is, too; but how much more important is the ministry of living faith, which must necessarily express and work with an evolving content? The Spirit is speaking to the Church today – at all levels – and therein lies its power to proclaim the Gospel and to point out the Way of Salvation.

If there is a special duty incumbent upon those who by profession are committed to the ministry of the Word, no Christian can excuse himself or herself from a similar task. I cannot wait around until I am spoon-fed. There are all too few ministers of the Gospel available to feed me. I will have a certain anemia in my faith if I attempted to depend wholly on others to feed me. And I cannot forget that I, too, have been baptized into the priesthood of Christ and confirmed as a mature Christian commissioned to witness to faith. I, too, must be a responsible student, making the consistent effort necessary to hear what the Spirit is saying to the Churches.

And the Spirit does not only speak to the Pope. It is not enough to regularly devour *Osservatore Romano.* He speaks among the People of God, He guides the faltering explorations of the theologians, He is at the meetings of bishops. I need to be open and sensitive to the overall movement that is going on, to have a mind and heart ready to move when it becomes clear in which direction the Spirit is leading. Fortunately we can rely on the Catholic press to help us here. Some of the Catholic papers – I think of Worcester's *Catholic Free Press,* to mention only one – regularly carry columns by competent theologians, explore controversial issues, report significant meetings and movements in the Church and in the Christian community at large. There are good periodicals that not only offer excellent articles but also summarize the field, like the "Moral Notes" in theological studies. With the help of some of these sources, according to our respective responsibilities, training, and capability, a regular weekly period of study can enable us to be sufficiently aware of the evolution that is taking place under the Spirit today.

B. Dialogical Reading

To stop at study, to turn all our sacred reading into study, would be missing the point. To "know" without having that knowledge become living knowledge, knowledge that is a source of love, would be rather futile – indeed, quite sterile. To use Cardinal Newman's very happy distinction, our notional assent has to become a real assent or there is no significant growth in faith taking place. The known content of faith needs to be interiorized, personalized, and this is another role of sacred reading.

Reading which is aiming at this kind of assimilation of faith could be called reflective reading or meditative reading. But I prefer to call it dialogical reading to underline the reality of what is taking place. It is not a question of going off in a corner with a book and chewing on it until we have made its convictions our own. Every word is a sacrament of the Word. This is preeminently true of the inspired words of Sacred Scripture, but also true of every other word we approach with faith. There is a Presence there who will speak to our hearts. We should approach this kind of reading more as a listener than as a reader.

In prayer we often tend to be quite monological – we don't let the Lord get a word in edgewise. And perhaps quite wisely – with the wisdom of the world – for if He does speak we can never be sure what He might say, what demands He might make upon us. But if we want to grow in faith we do have to let Him speak to us. We listen, and we do respond, though if we are wise disciples, we will do more listening and let our basic response be a docile heart, ready to hear the word, keep it, live it. "Speak, Lord, for your servant wants to hear."

I am going to return to this very important kind of reading, but let me, for the moment, pass on to the other types of reading.

C. Occasional Reading

There is another kind of reading I like to call occasional reading. It really is not another kind – it is dialogical reading done for the occasion.

As we move along in this life of faith we all have our difficulties. There are times of doubt and temptation. It may be a question of fidelity, of obedience, of chastity. A loved one has just disappeared from our life. The gross injustices of the world crash in on us. Sickness hits us. Or it may be that Mass has lost its meaning, or we just cannot seem to pray.

How are we to respond to these?

There is really only one way in which we can successfully respond to the trials and temptations of life, and that is out of faith. The faith-full person alone can adequately respond. "This is our victory – our faith, which has overcome the world." In these moments of darkness, we need the light of faith to show us the way, to guide us, to console us, to strengthen us. And where are we to find it? We may turn to a faith-full friend – the Divine Friend or another friend – and let him minister to us. We can do this in prayer – if it seems possible – or in a visit – if our faith-full friend is at home. Or we can do it in sacred reading.

Reading is perhaps the last thing we would think of doing when something is crushing us, yet it can be the source that will enable us to see through our tears and know there is an answer and a love present. It is good for us in our everyday reading to make a note of passages that really speak to us. Then in times of need we can revert to them. Some Bibles have helpful lists in them, indicating where we can find the passages that speak to particular needs. We are the heirs of a great and living tradition. Our fathers and mothers, through twenty centuries and more, have faced every sort of trial and have left us a tremendous wealth of shared faith. The Fathers of the Church, the great spiritual writers of the Middle Ages, and of our own times have touched upon just about every subject. We can turn to them and share their faith, conscious that they do, indeed, still live and care for us who are one with them in Christ. When I read Saint Bernard or William of St. Thierry to understand more the vicissitudes of my vocation, I am not listening to a page of cold print but to a living Father who speaks to me now in the Holy Spirit. Faith does come from such hearing, and the wherewithal to respond to this day's trial.

It is good to be mindful of this when it is our turn to speak the word of faith to a brother or sister who comes to us in an hour of need. We can only say so much to them, share so much of our little faith in prayer and word. But we can send our brother or sister off with a good book or article, and above all with the Sacred Scripture, which can continue to speak to their need and build up their faith.

Occasional reading is then dialogical reading done to meet the need of the occasion – something important to remember.

D. Lectio Divina

For the fourth kind of reading let me use a term consecrated by the centuries – not that that term could not and has not been used to refer to other kinds of reading – but because this is the kind of reading that comes from our age-old monastic traditions and properly belongs to the monk and the contemplative. It is nonetheless good for others to know about it. They can perhaps use it in times of retreat or sickness, when they have many hours to read, or perhaps when they are tired and their minds are ill-prepared for active reading.

This Lectio is a passive type of reading – indeed, a sort of contemplative prayer. In the other types of reading the mind is very active. It is seeking to learn, to understand, to assimilate, to develop convictions and motives. One can only do so much of that sort of activity. After a couple of hours of it – if not before – most minds tire.

In this passive sort of reading, though, we are not trying so much to understand or to motivate. We simply open ourselves to the word, seeking the experience of the Word Himself. We simply let the words flow in, knowing their sacramental power to quiet, to purify, to prepare the way for what Saint Bernard calls the "visits of the Word." Our desire, our intent is to receive such a visit. That is why such reading is indeed prayer. We are waiting on the Lord. He can and does, indeed, visit us in the course of other kinds of reading, but in this kind this is our whole intent. We just let the words gently flow in; we do not struggle with them. We wait in quietness of spirit. It is a kind of reading we can do when our minds are tired. We can do it for long stretches of time; it never tires. Rather, it refreshes.

Sometimes, perhaps more often than not, the Word does not seem to come. But later, as we are walking down the corridor, He meets us on the way. And life is wholly changed.

As I have said, this is the kind of active-passive reading most proper to the monks and nuns whose rule calls for long hours spent in Lectio Divina. But when one is enjoying the holy leisure of a retreat or must while away the hours in a sickbed, it can be a very fruitful way to spend some of the hours. Or perhaps it is the end of a long, busy day. The mind is tired, indeed. One does not feel like doing much of anything, but stands in need of some refreshment in the spirit. To pick up the Sacred Text – Scripture is usually best for this kind of reading – and let its powerful words gently flow in can be the beginning of a most revitalizing experience. Try it and see.

A LITTLE METHOD OR "TECHNIQUE"

For most of us, to establish something as a regular part of our lives and to be able to hand it on to others (hand on – that is what "tradition" is all about – and all of us who have been baptized into Christ and confirmed as Christians are called upon to share what we have received: "Freely have you received, freely give"), whether it be to brush our teeth or to pray and read, a little method, a few rules are usually very helpful, if not absolutely necessary. So I would like here to propose a simple method. I will refer explicitly to the hearing-reading of Sacred Scripture, but it can be applied equally to any kind of dialogical reading. This method is based in part on the prescriptions found in the Cistercian *Book of Regulations*, which spells out for the monk the tradition of centuries. When the monk comes to his reading he is told first to kneel, to invoke the Holy Spirit, to read the first words on his knees, and then to kiss the text before seating himself to continue his reading.

Rule One:
Take the Text with reverence and call upon Holy Spirit.

I do not think we can ever overemphasize the sacredness of the Scriptures. This is our great privilege: we are sons and daughters of the Book. God's Spirit has indeed been active among all men; His redeeming grace flows through the whole of the human family. One has only to meet some of the great roshis or swamis from the East to be very aware of this. Yet we, by a privilege we share in part with our Jewish kin, have been given something more. God in His astounding goodness and love has deigned to share with us, to reveal to us the secrets of His own inner life. "I no longer call you servants, but friends, because I make known to you all that the Father has made known to me."

The Church has always sought to show her great reverence for the Book. It has been copied and illuminated with the greatest care and magnificence. It has been bound in gold and silver, encrusted with gems. It has been carried solemnly in procession, incensed and reverenced. Craftsmen have executed beautiful stands for it, and magnificent ambos have been erected for its proclamation. It has a place of honor on the altar of sacrifice. And yet millions and millions of copies of it, big and small, have been printed, so no home, no pocket need be without it.

If you go into the church at Saint Joseph's Abbey, Spencer, Massachusetts – I am sure this is not the only place where this is true – you will see two lamps burning. One burns before the African-marble tabernacle, proclaiming the Real Presence within. The other hangs in the middle of the choir over the lectern on which the Sacred Text rests, proclaiming there, too, a Real Presence. For certainly the Presence in the Scriptures is not "unreal." It is real and powerful and efficacious. And if you were permitted to go about a monastery and look into the various rooms and the cells of the monks, again and again you would see the Sacred Text set apart in a place of honor, often a candle at its side.

The Bible is not a book to be just tossed on the desk, or put on the shelf with other books – one more in the row. It proclaims a Presence and love, and will do that in our own lives if we allow it to. Several people with whom I have shared these thoughts have told me how, after they had given the Sacred Text a special place in their room, it began to exert a meaningful influence in life, calling them regularly to prayer and reading. Try it and see!

The Bible evokes a Presence. So we begin our reading by an act of reverence – a bow, a kiss, kneeling or a full prostration – something that involves the body as well as the mind – bringing us effectively into that Presence; we take the text with reverence.

Then we call upon Holy Spirit. It was He who inspired the Chosen People, the early Christian community, the sacred writer, to set down this experience of faith. And it is He who lives in us to

teach us all. He is the fusing or coming into oneness
of these two activities of the Spirit that we now seek.

Rule Two:
For ten minutes we listen to the Lord and respond to Him.

Here an important element is that we read by time,
not by extent. We have been so schooled in speed
reading, our whole atmosphere is so charged with
the push to get going and get things done, that if we
decided to read a page or a chapter, there would be
a strong psychological push to rush on and get it
done. If we determine to read for ten minutes (and
who can say he is so busy he cannot find ten minutes
in the day to sit down with the Lord), no matter how
much or how little we cover, much of the pressure is
dissipated.

Really, though, it is not a question of reading; as
the rule says, it is a question of *listening*. If the first
word, the first sentence, speaks to us, we pause and
take time to savor it. We respond to it. We see how it
speaks to our present situation. Gently, leisurely, we
go on, listening, letting the Lord say what He wants to
say. The behavioral sciences tell us that when two
persons converse, only a small percentage of the
communication is in words. The whole of each person
speaks to the other, all the nonverbal communication
of body language and emotional climate. So, too, is it
in the communication with the Lord. The words we
receive from the text are only an outward sacrament,
as it were. The Presence speaks to us deeply. That is
why we can read the same text many successive days,
and each day the Lord will use it to say something
different. He speaks to us where we are.

Some days we might not get much beyond the first sentence or paragraph. Other days we might read right along. Nothing seems to speak to us for the moment. But then, later, as we share with another or go quietly about our work, one of the words will come alive in us. We take it as it comes, knowing that this daily meeting is important. And day by day He reveals to us more of Himself and of His teaching and we grow in faith.

Rule Three: Take a word with thanksgiving.

At the end of the appointed time (though we should not cut the time short, I would not hesitate to prolong it if He seems to want it) we take a moment to choose a word from all that He has said – somewhat as we do at the Liturgy of the Word – to carry with us. Some days there will be little question of choice. He will have spoken a particular word with such power that it will abide with us for days. Other days we will have to choose deliberately some word to keep with us, to ponder or to savor, a sort of koan, till our next meeting.

And we must thank Him. It is certainly an amazing thing that the very God of Heaven should be so willing to come and spend ten minutes with one of His little creations. A spirit of gratitude, a reflective appreciation of this, and an expression of it, helps us to be ever more faithful to the daily meeting. And, I am sure, encourages the Lord, if I may so speak, to be even more lavish in the light and insight He imparts.

As you can see, this is a very simple exercise, just enough method or "technique" to provide room for the free play of the Spirit. But let me guarantee, if you are faithful to this simple meeting with the Lord, it will change your life.

First of all, the Scriptures will become something very precious to you – a presence – whether enshrined in your room or in the pocket nearest your heart – preferably both. You will look forward to your daily reading. It will stretch out to longer periods and other times.

Secondly, more and more frequently, the Lord will speak to you, oftentimes from texts you have read so many, many times before. Recently I was listening to those first lines in Matthew. It was one of the older translations: "Abraham begot Isaac, Isaac begot Jacob, Jacob begot Judah and his brothers, Judah begot Perez and Zerah . . ." "Lord, I know you are a Jew and that all this is important for you. But what are you trying to say to me with all this begot, begot, begot?" "Read on," He replied. And so I read on: "Asa begot Jehosaphat, Jehosaphat begot Joram, Joram begot Uzziah . . ." "Really, Lord, what has all this begetting got to do with me?" Again He said, "Read on." And finally I came to: "Jacob begot Joseph, the husband of Mary, of whom Jesus was born." I must have heard that a hundred times before, but at that moment He spoke it, and I knew, as never before, that the very God did, indeed, become man, took my humanity, is truly one with me. I am sure the rest of my life will be different, richer, truer, because of the word He spoke to me in that moment. This is not a unique experience. It repeats itself again and again. Many have shared with me similar experiences. If you but seek and listen, the Lord will speak to you, too.

Thirdly, all your other reading-listening will be enlivened. The attitude and the fruit spill over to the whole of a life.

Fourthly, this will undoubtedly be true. If you continue daily in this encounter with Him, the Lord, deliberate sin will have no place in your life. It cannot. You cannot sit down regularly and look in the face of such a loving Lord and still continue to offend Him deliberately. One thing or another must go: the dialogical reading or the deliberate sin. There will still be sins of weakness. Human frailty remains with us. "The man [or woman] who says he is without sin is a liar." But we will know better than ever what an understanding Savior we have in Jesus, the Lord. And we will be able to be at peace, even in the midst of our sinfulness.

As our faith grows, as it is built up by these experiences, there grows up in us the desire to abide more and more in the depths of the faith reality, to live out of these depths, to experience a deeper union and communion with the loving Lord Whom this faith reveals and Who reveals this faith, and a desire to share all this goodness with others. We desire a deeper, more experiential prayer. We desire a deeper friendship, one in which we can share at these depths. In the following chapters we will pursue the fulfillment of these desires, again sharing practical ways or methods to do this.

TWO

Faith Experiencing

Centering Prayer • Prayer of Quiet

WE LIVE IN ONE OF THE GREATEST MOMENTS IN THE history of the human race. We live in the Christian era when God has sent His very own Son to bring us the fullest revelation of His Love and His inner Life and to share that Life with us. We live in the time of a Council, when there is a special outpouring of grace and light to enable the People of God to achieve a deeper and fuller insight into the Revelation. And certainly the Second Vatican Council was one of the more significant of the twenty Councils that the Lord has granted to His Church in the course of her twenty centuries of life. But over and beyond this, we live in the time of a second Pentecost. The humble Vicar of Christ, Pope John XXIII, dared to call upon the Father to send forth the Holy Spirit in that same powerful and unique way in which He did at the birth of Christianity. The Spirit is abroad now, among us as never before, enlivening us and calling us forth to ever fuller life. In a very real sense this is absolutely necessary. For the human family had made such strides forward that it is only by a real quickening of the Spirit that the Christian can hope to respond to the many new challenges of our times in a faith-full way.

One of the more significant changes for Western civilization, where Christianity largely resides, is the evolution from a conceptual era to an experiential one. Since Gutenberg's woodcuts first touched paper, the printed word and the ideas it disseminated more and more dominated Western culture. But in these last decades audiovisuals have led men to seek an ever fuller experience of reality. Technology's success has awakened desires; its failure to satisfy awakens deeper desires. The spirit of man has come alive in a way that now transcends cultures. And the man of the West finds that the stirring within him is the same as that which stirs within his brothers and sisters in what has been considered the "primitive" culture of the natives of many lands and in the more ancient cultures of the East.

The Christian who is nurtured in this climate is no longer content to ruminate on truths of dogma to develop motivating thoughts and feelings in an effort toward union with God. He wants to experience God as present, loving, and caring. And the Lord seems to be very willing to respond to this aspiration, which ultimately springs from His providential care of those whom His Love has created. I think this is the significance of the widespread charismatic movement. Among those who open themselves to the Spirit of God, He seems to be granting, in what is commonly referred to as the "Baptism of the Spirit," that kind of experience of Himself which the classical mystical writers have called a grace of union.

But not all are attracted to seek the experience of God in the enthusiastic and communicative climate that surrounds most charismatic groups. There are many who are drawn rather to seek this experience in the quiet of their own inner sanctuary where the Word dwells in His eternal stillness. There is ample evidence of this in the multitude of Christians who are flocking to the masters of the East to learn the methods of Zen and Yogic meditation, especially the transcendental meditation taught by Maharishi Mahesh Yogi.

TURNING TO THE EAST

A couple of years ago, I had occasion to visit a Ramakrishna temple in Chicago. Here I found twenty-four disciples gathered around a relatively young swami. The man was not unusually impressive, but he certainly lived what he taught and evidently spoke out of a personal inner experience. His disciples were an impressive group, twenty-two to fifty-five years of age. They expected another twenty-four to join them that year and were inaugurating a subsidiary ashram in nearby Michigan. All twenty-four were from Christian backgrounds. When I asked them what had drawn them to the temple, they invariably answered that they could find no one in their own Church who was willing to lead them into the deeper ways of the spirit where they could truly experience God. Then they met the swami and he was willing to do that. They still worshipped Christ, but now unfortunately as only one of many incarnations of God. In their search they have somewhat lost their way because there was no Christian master (or, to be more faithful to our own traditional terminology, no Spiritual Mother or Father) ready to guide them, sharing with them from the fullness of his own lived experience.

Over the years in retreat work I have talked to many, many priests and religious. I have found that in most cases, though not all, in the seminary or the novitiate they have been taught methods of prayer and active meditation. In many cases they have also had a course in ascetical and mystical theology in which they have heard about the various stages of contemplative prayer. Unfortunately they have usually been left with the impression or have been actually taught that it is a very rare sort of thing, usually found only in enclosed monasteries. To seek it is presumptuous. One must plug away faithfully at active meditation and perhaps someday, in the far distant future, after long years of fidelity, God might give one this precious but rare gift of contemplative prayer. In no instance have I yet found anyone who had been taught in the seminary or the novitiate a simple method for entering into passive meditation or contemplative prayer.

This is sad. Especially in face of the fact that Saint Teresa of Avila had taught that those who were faithful to prayer could expect in a relatively short time – six months or a year – to be led into a prayer of quiet. Dom Marmion believed that by the end of his novitiate a religious was usually ready for contemplative prayer. One of the signs that Saint John of the Cross pointed to as an indication that one is ready for contemplative prayer is that active meditation no longer works – an experience very many priests and religious do have. Faced with this experience, and with no one showing them how to move on to contemplative prayer, many give up regular prayer. A faithful few plug on, sometimes for years, in making painful meditations that are anything but refreshing. Given this state of affairs it is not surprising that Christians seeking help to enter into the quiet, inner experience of God find little among their priests and religious.

We know that if a person desiring to seek the experience of God in deep meditation does go on to one of the many swamis found in the West today, he or she will be quickly taught a simple method to pursue this goal. "Sit this way. Hold your hands this way. Breathe thus. Say this word in this manner. Do this twice a day for so many minutes." And if the recipient does this, he or she usually has very good experiences. We can see this, up to a point, as a good thing. For often, whether the person knows His name or not, he or she is in fact seeking God. And in carrying through this exercise, devoting mind and heart to this pursuit, he is actually engaging in a very pure form of prayer. The sad part of it is that his pursuit and his experience, probably of God's very real presence in him in His creative love, is not informed by faith. Sadder still is the fact that, in not a few cases, grateful recipients, so helped by the swami's meditation technique, begin to accept from him, also, his philosophy of life, abandoning their Christian heritage. Some of the greater swamis, such as Swami Satichidananda and Maharishi Mahesh Yogi, certainly advise against this, but such advice can fall on ears deafened by an almost cultic veneration for a truly selfless master.

These good masters from the East are truly a challenge, whether they intend to be or not, and in more ways than one. For one thing they certainly remind us that the effective teacher, at least in the area of life-giving teaching, must be one who lives what he teaches. To try to teach the Christian Gospel with its strong bias for the poor and its way of daily abnegation – "If you would be my disciple, take up your cross daily [not monthly or weekly, my novice master would say with emphasis, but daily] and come follow me" – while busily pursuing the same pleasures and immediate goals pursued by the worldly materialist is to condemn oneself to a fruitless ministry. We must teach more by what we do, what we live, than by what we say, if we want our hearers to take us seriously.

The swamis' response to seekers makes us ask ourselves, Are there not in our own Christian tradition some simple methods, some meditation "techniques," which we can use to enter into quiet, contemplative union with God? Before responding, I would like to say we Christians should not hesitate to make use of the good techniques that our wise friends from the East are offering, if we find them, in fact, helpful. As Saint Paul said: "All things are yours, and you are Christ's, and Christ is God's." We should not hesitate to take the fruit of the age-old wisdom of the East and "capture" it for Christ. Indeed, those of us who are in ministry should make the necessary effort to acquaint ourselves with as many of these Eastern techniques as possible. Not that we will necessarily find them useful in our own prayer seeking, though this might well be the case, but that we might be prepared to enter into intelligent dialogue with Eastern spiritual masters and, more important, that we might be prepared to help our fellow Christians, who do learn these techniques and find them helpful, to integrate them into their Christian faith experience. I think it is a fact that many Christians who take their prayer life seriously have been greatly helped by Yoga, Zen, TM, and similar practices, especially where they have been initiated by reliable teachers and have a solidly developed Christian faith to give inner form and meaning to the resulting experiences. (See Chapter Five.)

But to return to our question: do we have, in our Christian tradition, simple methods or techniques for entering into contemplative prayer? Yes, we certainly do. Some might draw back at this statement. The idea of using a "technique" to communicate with God, Whom we have the privilege of knowing personally, seems repulsive. And to expect to attain to contemplation by a "technique" smacks of Pelagianism. So let me explain.

THE USE OF "TECHNIQUE"

First of all, "techniques," methods, are certainly not foreign to the prayer experience of the average Catholic. The rosary is a "technique" – and certainly not one to be readily discounted. It has led many, many Christians to deep contemplative union with

God. The Stations of the Cross are another "technique." So are the Ignatian Exercises, which are directly ordered to contemplation. Well enough known in the West today, at least by name and reputation, is the ancient Eastern Christian technique of the Jesus Prayer. We have, in fact, many Christian techniques.

The use of a technique or method in prayer to help us come into contact with God present to us, in us, and to bring our whole selves into quietness to enjoy that presence and be refreshed by it, is certainly not, in itself, Pelagian. Mystical theologians have not hesitated to speak of an "acquired contemplation" – in distinction to "infused contemplation" – a contemplative state or experience which the contemplator has taken some part in bringing into being. All prayer is a response to God and begins with Him. To deny this would be Pelagian. God's grace is not operative only in infused contemplation. When the little child lisps his "Now I lay me down to sleep . . ." if there is any movement of faith and love there, any true prayer, grace is present and operative. Every prayer is a response to a movement of grace, whether we are explicitly aware of it or not, whether we consciously experience the movement, the call, the attraction, or not. God present in us, present all around us, is calling us to respond to His presence, His love, His caring. We are missing reality if we think otherwise.

When we use a technique, a method, to pray, we are doing so because God's grace, to which we are freely responding, is efficaciously inviting us to do this. That we have been taught the technique and have responded to the teaching is all His grace at work, inviting us, leading us, guiding us to have a deeper experience of our union with Him. That is why it takes a certain courage – or foolhardiness – to learn such a technique. For it is, indeed, an invitation from the Lord to enter and abide within. Not to respond to such a loving invitation from the infinite God of love is sheer tragedy. Yet, to respond to such an invitation is to open oneself to a transformation of conscience and consciousness, with all that that can lead to. One's life will never be the same again.

THE PRAYER OF *THE CLOUD*

Yes, we do have in our Christian tradition simple methods, "techniques," for entering into contemplative prayer, a prayer of quiet. And without more ado I would like to share one such method with you. The one I have chosen is drawn from a little book called *The Cloud of Unknowing*. This is indeed a popular book in our time. At present it is available in four different paperback editions. (The one edited by William Johnston and published by Doubleday Image Books is the best.) The author is an unknown English Catholic writer of the fourteenth century. He could hardly have put his name to the work, for all that he teaches belongs to the common heritage of the Christian community.

At the time of our author's writing there was a vibrant spirituality alive and widespread in the Christian West. The swell had begun with the great

Gregorian reform in the eleventh century and the ensuing monastic revival. The great Cistercian abbeys of the twelfth century often housed only eighty or ninety or a hundred monks, but had two, three, four hundred, or more, lay brothers who labored in the granges, opening up new land or developing sheep runs, or who were active in the markets and agricultural trading centers. These men were not unlike the figure of the staretz made familiar to us by the novels of Dostoevski. While they shared their agricultural concerns with the hired help, the neighboring peasants and serfs, or sold their wool in the markets, they did not fail to share at the same time something of their spiritual awareness and their simple ways of prayer. These holy men were followed by the enthusiastic sons of Saint Francis and the other mendicants. All, even the poorest, the most illiterate, the villainous, were invited to intimacy with the Lord. The fourteenth century was a high tide for the Christian spirit in the West.

Unfortunately it would soon enough ebb. With the Reformation, the monastic centers of spiritual life would be swept away by the new currents that flowed through much of Europe. And on the rest of the Continent the prosecution of Quietism and Illuminism by an overly zealous and defensive Inquisition would send contemplation to hide fearfully in the corners of a few convents and monasteries. A great movement of the Christian spirit flowed away with the undercurrent, only to surface and return under the impulsion of the mighty winds of a second Pentecost. These winds blow across the face of the whole earth. They certainly are not contained by the Church. But the Church, the Christian community, cannot afford to be slow to respond to them. True renewal must begin with each Christian responding to the call of the Spirit within, to the call to the center where God dwells, waiting to refresh, revitalize, renew.

This simple method of entering into contemplative prayer has been aptly called "centering prayer." The name is inspired by Thomas Merton. In his writings he stressed that the only way to come into contact with the living God is to go to one's center and from there pass into God. This is the way the author of *The Cloud* would lead us, although his imagery is somewhat different.

The simple method he teaches really belongs to the common heritage of man. I remember on one occasion describing it to a teacher of transcendental meditation. He replied, "Why, that's TM." I could not agree with him. There are very significant differences, but perhaps it takes faith really to perceive them. (See Chapter Four.) I can also remember, when I was in Greece a couple of years ago, finding a Greek translation of *The Cloud of Unknowing*. The late archbishop of Corinth had written the introduction. In it he stated that this was the work of an unknown fourteenth-century English Orthodox writer. He was certain it belonged to his Christian tradition.

If one reads *The Cloud of Unknowing* on one's own, as perhaps many of my readers have, one is not apt effectively to draw from the text the simple technique the author offers. This is not to be

wondered at. One will have the same experience
reading books on the Jesus Prayer. As the Spiritual
Fathers on Mount Athos pointed out to me, no
Spiritual Father would seek to teach this method of
prayer by a book. It is meant to be handed on
personally – tradition. The writings are but to
support the learner in his experience and help him
place the practice in the full context of his life. This,
too, I believe is the case with *The Cloud of Unknowing*.
Simply reading it will not usually teach the method.
But one practicing the method will certainly draw
encouragement and understanding from reading the
text. This is not to deny the inherent difficulty of
reading a writing that comes out of the living
Christian culture of six centuries ago. If we were to
try to take all the strong pious statements of the
author as prosaic twentieth-century factual writing,
no Christian with one whit of humility would deem
himself worthy of approaching this prayer. The
author's poetic imagery might also put us off. Yet the
rich, perennially valid substance is there. And
anyone living in the tradition and sharing the
experience quickly perceives this.

At this point I find in myself certain hesitancies,
realizing, on the one hand, the need for more simple,
concrete instruction, and on the other, questioning
the wisdom of trying to hand this on through the
written word, acting in a sense contrary to the
traditional way of the Fathers. Yet the desire today
is so widespread, the teachers so few, that it seems
prudent to risk the endeavor, relying on Holy Spirit,
the true and only Master, immediately present to the

reader, to translate the printed word into something living that can engender true life.

And so now let me try to spell out the "technique" of *The Cloud of Unknowing* a little more concretely, adding some practical advice and explanation. To do this I would like to sum up the method in three rules. Every time I say that, I imagine I hear our humble author turning over gently in his grave. To give rules is the last thing he probably would ever have thought of doing. But we practical twentieth-century folk will probably find putting the method into rules or guidelines will facilitate our use of it and our ability to pass it on to others.

POSTURE AND RELAXATION

But first let me say a word about posture. Some wonderful ways of sitting have come to us from the East. They are ideal for meditation. But unless we are long practiced, and in most cases, have gotten an early start, our muscles and bones do not too readily adapt themselves to these postures. I think for most of us Westerners the best posture for prayer is to be comfortably settled in a good chair – one that gives firm support to the back, but at the same time is not too hard or stiff. As the author of *The Cloud* says, "simply sit relaxed and quiet . . ." (c. 44).

We do not want to get too comfortably settled or the body will receive the signal that it is time for sleep. The back is most comfortable when it is straight and well supported. The head should be settled comfortably on its own, not leaning back on anything. If we should perceive it has fallen forward during the prayer (not an uncommon experience) it is good to bring it back up. For if it leans far forward it can inhibit breathing and put a strain on neck and back muscles.

Most important, the body should be relaxed. When our Lord said, "Come to me all you who labor and are heavily burdened, and I will refresh you," He meant the whole person, body, soul and spirit – not just the spirit. But the body is not apt to be refreshed if we begin the prayer physically tense. Sitting rigidly for thirty minutes or shifting about, distractedly seeking comfort, will probably result in only more tenseness. It is similar to sleep. If we go to sleep with the body tensed, we will wake up not rested but only more tense and tired. It is important then as we settle in our chairs for prayer that we take what time we need to relax. Perhaps some will want to employ some exercises. This is good if they will help us to be more relaxed as we pray.

Settling down in our chair and letting go, letting the chair fully support the body, is sacramental of what is to take place in the prayer. In centering prayer we settle in God, let ourselves go, let Him fully support us, rest us, refresh us.

Posture and relaxation are important. It is good, too, if we close our eyes during this prayer. It is true, some techniques like Zen call for keeping the eyes open. But these are usually effortful techniques. This method, however, is effortless; it is a letting go. "It is simply a spontaneous desire springing suddenly toward God (*The Cloud*, c. 4). And the more we can gently eliminate outside disturbances the better.

That is why it is good, if possible, to make this prayer in a quiet place, a place apart, though this is not essential. More important is that it be a situation in which we will not be disturbed in the course of the meditation. I have meditated this way in airports – certainly not quiet places, but no one will ordinarily disturb you as you sit there among the many waiting passengers. Quiet, though, will usually be found helpful. Psychologically, also, it is experienced as helpful if one has a sort of special place for meditation – a place apart, even though the "apart" may be only a corner of a room where there is a presence sacramentalized in Bible, icon, or sacred image, and the going apart involves swinging around in our chair from desk to shrine. The physical setup and the bodily movement reinforce the sense of passing now from the frenetic activities of the day to a deeper state of prayerful rest and divine refreshment.

THREE RULES

But now let us get on with the "rules" for entering into centering prayer – the prayer of quiet contemplation.

Rule One:

> At the beginning of the prayer we take a mo-ment or two to quiet down and then move in faith to God dwelling in our depths; and at the end of the prayer we take several minutes to come out, mentally praying the Our Father.

So, once we are settled down in our chair and relaxed, we enter into a short period of silence. Sixty seconds can initially seem like a long time when we are doing nothing and are used to being constantly on the go. Better to take a little more time rather than less. Then we move in faith to God, Father, Son, and Holy Spirit, dwelling in creative love in the depths of our being. This is the whole essence of the prayer. "Center all your attention and desire on him and let this be the sole concern of your mind and heart" (*The Cloud*, c. 3). Faith moving toward its Object in hope and love – this is the whole of the theological, the Christian life. All the rest of the method is simply a means to enable us to abide quietly in this center and to allow our whole being to share in this refreshing contact with its Source.

Faith is fundamental for this prayer, as for any prayer. We will have no desire to enter into union and communion, to pray, if we do not have at least some glimmer in faith of the All-Lovable, the All-Desirable. But it is essentially a "wonderful work of love," a total response to Him Who is known by living faith.

THE INNER PRESENCE

When God makes things, He does not just put them together and toss them out there, to let them fly along in His creation. "One is good – God." And One is true, and beautiful, and all being – our God. And everything else is only insofar as it here and now actively participates in Him and shares His being. At every moment God is intimately present to each and every particle of His creation, sharing with it, in creative love, His very own being. And so, if we really see this paper, we do not just see the paper, but we see God bringing it into being and sustaining it in being. We perceive the Divine presence.

If this is true of all the other elements, how much more true is it for the greatest of God's creation – the human person, made to His own very image and likeness. When we go to our depths we find not only the image of God, but God Himself, bringing us forth in His creative love. We go to our center and pass from there into the present God.

Yet there is still something even more wonderful here for the Christian. We have been baptized into Christ. We are in some very real, though mysterious way, Christ, the Son of God, the Second Person of the Blessed Trinity. "I live, now not I, but Christ lives in me." As we go to the depths we realize in faith our identity with Christ the Son. And even now, with Him and in Him, we come forth from the Father in the eternal generation, and return to the Father in that perfect Love which is Holy Spirit. What prayer! This is really stupendous, beyond adequate conception. Yet our faith tells us it is so. It is part of that whole reality that revelation has opened up to us. And it is for us to take possession of it. We have been made sharers in the Divine nature by Baptism. We have been given the *Gift* of the Holy Spirit. We have but to enter into what is ours, what we truly are.

And that is what we do in this prayer. In a movement of faith that is hope and love, we go to the center and turn ourselves over to God in a simple being there, in a presence that is perfect and complete adoration, response, love, and "Amen" to that movement that we are in the Son to the Father.

COMING OUT OF CONTEMPLATION

In this prayer we go very deep into ourselves. Some speak of a fourth state of consciousness, a state beyond waking, sleeping, or dreaming states. Tests have shown that meditators do achieve a state of rest which is deeper than that attained in sleep. Have you ever had the experience of suddenly being rudely awakened out of very deep sleep? It is rather jarring, to say the least. We do not want to come out of contemplative prayer in a jarring way. Rather we want to bring its deep peace into the whole of our life. That is why we prescribe taking several minutes coming out, moving from the level of deep, self-forgetful contemplation to silent awareness and then a conscious interior prayer before moving out into full activity. When the time we have determined to pray is up, we stop using the prayer word, savor the silence, the Presence, for a bit, and then begin interiorly to pray the Our Father.

I suggest saying the Our Father. It is a perfect prayer, taught us by the Lord Himself. We gently let the successive phrases come to mind. We savor them, enter into them. What matter if in fact it takes a good while. It is a beginning of letting our contemplative prayer flow out into the rest of our prayer life.

The best time for meditating seems to be in the early morning, after we freshen up, and in the early evening before supper. But this is something each one has to work out for himself. Right after eating seems a poor time. One's center is someplace else! Nor is it good to take a stimulant, like coffee, just before "centering." That is rather like trying to go in two directions at once.

SLEEP

It might be good to say a few words here about sleep and meditation, for it is to avoid sleep that we are tempted to take coffee or the like before praying. If we have not prayed in this deep way before, we are apt to wonder if we have not fallen asleep. Saint Teresa of Avila in her *Interior Castle* tells us that "in the prayer of quiet . . . until the soul has gained much experience, it doubts what really happened to it. 'Was it nothing but fancy, or was it asleep? Did it come from God . . .' The mind feels a thousand misgivings" (Bk. 5, c. 1, no. 5). We pass beyond self-awareness. The prayer is deeply restful. At the end all we can recall is a certain period of blankness. The nearest experience like this we have previously known is that of sleep. Yet somehow we are usually quite aware that we have not been sleeping.

However, it certainly is possible to fall asleep meditating. The author of *The Cloud* has some consoling words for us. He tells us not to worry if we do fall asleep, even to thank God. Our Father loves us as much when we are asleep as when we are awake. If we do doze in the midst of this work of love, we will probably awaken rather quickly. It is good then to return simply to our prayer. It will usually be a very good prayer, for we are now relaxed and rested.

However, if we are regularly falling asleep during our prayer, we should perhaps ask ourselves some questions. Maybe the Lord is trying to say something to us. Maybe we are simply not getting enough sleep. This is a common failure among dedicated people. And there is a subtle bit of pride usually lurking in it. We are trying to do more than we should. "If the Lord does not build the house, in vain the masons toil . . . in vain you get up earlier and put off going to bed, sweating to make a living, since He provides for His beloved as they sleep." We belong to the Lord, and so should do what He wants us to do – no more and no less.

Our falling asleep may simply be due to the fact that we are getting too comfortable. The body is getting the signal to sleep. We need to try, perhaps, a more upright, somewhat less comfortable chair.

Or again, this falling asleep may be telling us we really do not want to enter into deep union and communion with God. Perhaps we are afraid. Perhaps we are just not that interested – we do not yet know Him enough. The remedy is faith building – getting to know Him in all His lovableness and desirability, to love Him enough to be willing to risk the demands His intimate love will put upon us.

A VALUABLE ASCETICISM

We strongly recommend two periods of contemplative prayer in the course of a day. It introduces into our day a good rhythm: a period of deep rest and refreshment in the Lord flowing out into eight or ten hours of activity, and then another period of renewal to carry us through what is for most today a long evening of activity. This is certainly much better than trying to base sixteen hours of activity on the morning prayer.

Twenty minutes seems to be a good period to start with. Less than this hardly gives one a chance to get fully into the prayer and be wholly refreshed. Some will feel themselves drawn to extend the period to twenty-five or thirty minutes or perhaps thirty-five. On a day of retreat or when we are sick in bed, and our activity is curtailed, we can easily add more periods of contemplative prayer. This might be better than prolonging individual periods. Those who are generally living a contemplative life may find somewhat longer periods helpful.

For most, the real asceticism of this form of prayer comes in scheduling into our daily life two periods for it. Once we are going full steam, it is difficult to stop, drop everything, go apart and simply be to the Lord. And yet there is a tremendous value here.

All of us theoretically subscribe to the words quoted above, "If the Lord does not build the house, in vain the masons toil." But in practice most of us work as though God could not possibly get things done if we did not do them for Him. The fact is there is nothing that we are doing that God could not raise up a stone in the field to do for Him. The realization of this puts us in our true place. Though, lest we do get too knocked down by such a realization of our insignificance, let me hasten to add that there is one thing that we alone can do for God. And that is the one thing for which He created us, and which gives us our infinite importance and worth, and that one thing is to give Him our personal love. No one else can give God our personal love. It is uniquely for this that He created us. This is our great significance. The very God of Heaven and earth wants, and needs because He wants, our personal love.

I have run into a situation in marriage counseling a number of times. The couple is unhappy. The wife is dissatisfied and the husband cannot see why. He goes into a long recital of all he is doing for her. He is holding down two or three jobs, building a new house, buying her everything. But to all this the wife quietly replies: if only he would stop for a few minutes and give me himself! I sometimes think that God, as He sees us rushing about in all our doing of good, says to Himself: if only they would stop for a few minutes and give me themselves!

Yes, we theoretically subscribe to the fact that God is the principal agent. But we push frenetically on. Nothing can help us so much as to get a real grasp on the fact of God's allness in our accomplishments – and the peace and freedom that come from such practical realization – as actually stopping regularly and letting God take care of things. He really can. We can trust Him to manage His world for twenty minutes without us while we meditate – and not mess it up too much!

And if, while we pray, someone has to wait at our door for ten or fifteen minutes, he or she will probably learn a lot about prayer while waiting – certainly more than if inside listening to us talk about prayer. Actions speak louder than words. Those around us will not fail to notice, even though we might prefer they would not, when we begin to give prayer prime time in our busy lives.

TIME

It is important to be faithful to the time we set for our prayer. When we determine to contemplate for twenty minutes we should faithfully stay with it for the full twenty minutes and not cut corners when work is pressing or the thoughts and tensions are many. It is at such times we most need this refreshing time with the Lord. And it may take all of the twenty minutes to reestablish our needed inner peace.

A question frequently asked is, How is one to tell when time is up? If we contemplate regularly for the same amount of time, we will soon find that we come out automatically at the determined time. At first, however, that will not be the case. What we do is when the question comes to mind, Is it time? we just take a quick look at our watch. If it is time, we close our eyes and begin slowly to come out of the prayer. If it is not yet time, we gently resume our prayer word and go on with the meditation.

Rule Two:

> After resting for a bit in the center in faithful
> love, we take up a single, simple word that
> expresses this response and begin to let it repeat
> itself within.

As the author of *The Cloud* puts it: "If you want to
gather all your desire into one simple word that the
mind can easily retain, choose a short word rather than
a long one. A one-syllable word such as 'God' or 'love'
is best. But choose one that is meaningful to you. Then
fix it in your mind so that it will remain there, come
what may . . . Be careful in this work and never strain
your mind or imagination, for truly you will not succeed
this way. Leave these faculties at peace" (c. 7, 4).

What we are concerned with here is a simple,
effortless prolongation or abiding in the act of faith –
love – presence. This is so simple, so effortless, so
restful, that it is a bit subtle and so needs some explanation. A spiritual act is an instantaneous act, an act
without time. "The will needs only this brief fraction
of a moment to move toward the object of its desire"
(*The Cloud*, c. 4). As soon as we move in love to God
present in the depths, we are there. There a perfect prayer
of adoration, love, and presence is. And we simply want
to remain there and be what we are: Christ responding to
the Father in the perfect Love, the Holy Spirit.

To facilitate our abiding quietly there, and to
bring our whole being as much as possible to rest in
this abiding, after a brief experience of silent
presence we take up a single simple word that
expresses for us our faith-love movement. We have
seen the author of *The Cloud* suggests such words as

"God" or "love." A vocative word seems usually to be best. We begin very simply to let this word repeat itself within us. We let it take its own pace, louder or softer, faster or slower; it may even fuzz out into silence. "For it is best when this word is wholly interior without a definite thought or actual sound" (*The Cloud,* c. 40).

We might think of it as if the Lord Himself, present in our depths, were quietly repeating His own name, evoking His presence and very gently summoning us to an attentive response. We are quite passive. We let it happen. "Let this little word represent to you God in all His fullness and nothing less than the fullness of God. Let nothing except God hold sway in your mind and heart" (*The Cloud,* c. 40).

The subtle thing here is the effortlessness. We are so used to being very effortful. We are a people out to succeed, to accomplish, to do. It is hard for us to let go and let God do. And, after all, if we do, if we expend great effort, then when it is done we can pat ourselves on the back and salute ourselves for our great accomplishment. This prayer leaves no room for pride. We have but to let go and let it be done unto us according to His revealed Word. The temptation for us is to change the quiet mental repetition of the prayer word, which simply prolongs a state of being present, into an effortful repetition of an ejaculation and to use it energetically to knock out any thoughts or "distractions" that come along. This brings us to our third rule.

Rule Three:

Whenever in the course of the prayer we become aware of anything else, we simply, gently return to the prayer word.

I want to emphasize that word *aware.* Unfortunately we are not able to turn off our minds and imaginations by the flick of a switch. Thoughts and images keep coming in a steady stream. "No sooner has a man turned toward God in love when through human frailty he finds himself distracted by the remembrance of some created thing or some daily care. But no matter. No harm done; for such a person quickly returns to deep recollection" (*The Cloud*, c. 4).

In this prayer we go below the thoughts and images offered by the mind and imagination. But at times they will grab at our attention and try to draw it away from the restful Presence. This is because these thoughts or images refer to something that has a hold on us, something we fear, or desire, or are in some other way intensely involved with. When we become aware of these thoughts, if we continue to dwell on them, we leave our prayer and become involved again in the tensions. But if, at the moment of awareness, we simply, gently return to our prayer word (thus implicitly renewing our act of presence in faith-full love), the thought or image with its attendant tension will be released and flow out of our lives. And we will come into a greater freedom and peace that will remain after our prayer is over.

Should some thought go on annoying you, demanding to know what you are doing, answer with this one word alone. If your mind

begins to intellectualize over the meaning and
connotation of this little word, remind yourself
that its value lies in its simplicity. Do this and I
assure you these thoughts will vanish. (*The
Cloud of Unknowing,* c. 7)

We can see how pure this prayer is. In active
forms of prayer we use thoughts and images as
sacraments and means for reaching out to God. In
this prayer we go beyond them, we leave them
behind, as we go to God Himself abiding in our
depths. It is a very pure act of faith. Perhaps in this
prayer we will for the first time really act in pure
faith. So often our faith is leaning on the concepts
and images of faith. Here we go beyond them to the
Object Himself of faith, leaving all the concepts and
images behind.

We can see, too, how Christian this prayer is. For
we very truly die to ourselves, our more superficial
selves, the level of our thoughts, images, and
feelings, in order to live to Christ, to enter into our
Christ-being in the depths. We "die" to all our
thoughts, and imaginings, no matter how beautiful
they may be or how useful they might seem. We
leave them all behind, for we want immediate
contact with God Himself, and not some thought,
image, or vision of Him – only the faith experience
of Himself. "You are to concern yourself with no
creature whether material or spiritual nor with their
situation or doings whether good or ill. To put it
briefly, during this work you must abandon them
all . . ." (*The Cloud,* c. 5).

"BY THEIR FRUITS . . ."

There is another consequence of this transcending of thought and image. This prayer cannot be judged in itself. As it goes beyond thought, beyond image, there is nothing left by which to judge it. In active meditation, at the end we can make some judgments. I had some good thoughts, I felt some good affections, I had lots of distractions, etc. But all that is irrelevant to this prayer. If we have lots of thoughts – good, lots of tension is being released. If we have few thoughts – good, there was no need for them. The same for feelings, images, etc. All these are purely accidental; they do not touch the essence of the prayer, which goes on in all its purity, whether these be present or not. There is nothing left by which to judge the prayer in itself. If we simply follow the three rules, the prayer is always good, no matter what we think or feel.

There is, however, one way in which the goodness of this prayer is confirmed for us. Our Lord has said, "You can judge a tree by its fruits." If we are faithful to this form of prayer, making it a regular part of our day, we very quickly come to discern – and often others discern it in us even more quickly – the maturing in our lives of the fruits of the Spirit – love, joy, peace, patience, benignity, kindness, gentleness – all the fruits of the Spirit. I have experienced this in my own life and I have seen this again and again in the lives of others, sometimes in a most remarkable way. What happens, the way the Spirit seems to bring this about, is that in this prayer we experience not only our oneness with God in Christ but also our oneness with all the rest of the

Body of Christ, and indeed with the whole of
creation, in God's creative love and sharing of being.
Thus we begin, connaturally as it were, to experience
the presence of God in all things, the presence of
Christ in each person we meet. Moreover, we sense
a oneness with them. From this flows a true
compassion – a "feeling with." This contemplative
prayer, far from removing us from others, makes us
more and more conscious of our oneness with them.
Love, kindness, gentleness, patience grow. Joy and
peace, too, in the pervasive presence of God's caring
love in all. Contemplative prayer helps us take
possession of our real transcendent relationship
with God in Christ, as well as our real relationship
with each and every person in Christ.

I have written enough, and more than enough, on
three simple rules, and perhaps you are eager now
to take them up and begin to meditate. So let me
simply recapitulate them here:

> *Rule One:* At the beginning of the prayer we take
> a minute or two to quiet down and then move
> in faith to God dwelling in our depths; and at
> the end of the prayer we take several minutes to
> come out, mentally praying the Our Father (or
> some other prayer).

> *Rule Two:* After resting for a bit in the center in
> faith-full love, we take up a single, simple word
> that expresses this response and begin to let it
> repeat itself within.

> *Rule Three:* Whenever in the course of the prayer
> we become aware of anything else, we simply
> return to the prayer word.

May these simple rules prove to be for you, and all those with whom you share them, a gentle, loving invitation from the Lord to a fuller, richer, deeper life in Him, a life marked by the fruits of the Holy Spirit.

AN ADDED NOTE

When a number are praying together – and some find this very supportive – it is helpful if one takes the lead. After everyone is settled, the leader opens the prayer, articulating the act of faith. At the end he or she recites the Lord's Prayer aloud. The opening prayer might go something like this:

> Lord, we worship You as our very God. We believe You are truly in our depths. We come to You in adoration and love. Draw us, bring us into Yourself. Refresh us and renew us. We come to You, Lord. We give ourselves wholly to You. We come, O Lord, we come.

I think it is important – certainly very helpful – when we are teaching this simple method of prayer to others that, after we have explained the three rules, we actually pray with them. If it is at all possible, it would be good to meet with them several times in the course of the following week to pray again with them. Let there be plenty of time for questions and sharing about the experience. As we have pointed out above, and will develop in a later chapter, such sharing is faith building and confirming. And faith is the absolutely essential starting point for all prayer and all Christian life.

THREE

Centering Prayer

Merton • Abhishiktananda • Van Kaam

IN A TIME WHEN THE SPIRIT IS ENLIVENING THE consciousness of all of good will and calling the Christian community to true renewal it is not surprising to find many spiritual writers articulating the call to contemplation. I would like to share some excerpts from a few of the great spiritual masters of our times which in various ways re-echo, with contemporary insight, the teaching of *The Cloud*, which I have tried to share in the last chapter.

THOMAS MERTON (FATHER LOUIS, O.C.S.O.)

I believe most will agree that the greatest Spiritual Father the West has known in our times is the Cistercian monk, Father Louis Merton, better known by his baptismal name of Thomas. Not only did he personally direct the spiritual formation of the largest contemplative community in the West, but through his writings, which are still being translated and published in many languages, he continues to engender life in the hearts of men and women throughout Christendom and beyond.

As is well known, in the last days of his earthly life, Father Louis set out on a pilgrimage to the East to share with spiritual masters in India, Thailand, Japan, and elsewhere. On the eve of his departure from the United States he spent a few days of quiet sharing with friends at Redwoods Abbey in California. Br. David Steindl-Rast, who had the grace of being with him at that time, gathered up some of Father Louis' final words. To our own point, Father Louis said:

> It's a risky thing to pray, and the danger is that our very prayers get between God and us. The great thing in prayer is not to pray, but to go directly to God. If saying your prayers is an obstacle to prayer, cut it out. Let Jesus pray. Thank God Jesus is praying. Forget yourself. Enter into the prayer of Jesus. Let him pray in you . . . The best way to pray is: stop. Let prayer pray within you, whether you know it or not. This means a deep awareness of our true inner identity . . . But the point is that we need not justify ourselves. By grace we are Christ. Our relationship with God is that of Christ to the Father in the Holy Spirit. (*Thomas Merton, Monk*, Image Books, pp. 89-90)

I think that expresses well what is at the heart of centering prayer. As I mentioned above, the very expression "centering prayer" derives from Father Merton's teaching. Let me then just share a number of quotes from his many published works.

> Unless we discover this deep self, which is hidden with Christ in God, we will never really know ourselves as persons. Nor will we know

God. For it is by the door of this deep self that
we enter into the spiritual knowledge of God.
(And indeed, if we seek our true selves it is not
in order to contemplate ourselves but to pass beyond ourselves and find Him.) (*The New Man*, p.
32)

The fact is, however, that if you descend into the
depths of your own spirit . . . and arrive
somewhere near the center of what you are, you
are confronted with the inescapable truth that,
at the very root of your existence, you are in
constant and immediate and inescapable
contact with the infinite power of God. (*The
Contemplative Life*, p. 28)

. . . an immediate existential union with Him in
our souls as the source of our physical life. (*The
New Man*, p. 84)

. . . an immediate existential union with the
Triune God as the source of the grace and virtue
in our spirit. (Ibid., p. 85)

This perfect union is not a fusion of natures but
a unity of love and of experience. The distinction
between the soul and God is no longer
experienced as a separation into subject and
object when the soul is united to God. (*Thomas
Merton Reader*, p. 515)

It starts, not from the thinking and self-aware
subject . . . Underlying the subjective experience
of the individual self there is the immediate
experience of Being. This is totally different
from an experience of self-consciousness. It is
completely non-objective. It has in it none of the

split and alienation that occurs when the subject becomes aware of itself as a quasi-object. The consciousness of Being . . . is an immediate experience that goes beyond reflexive awareness. It is not "consciousness of" but pure consciousness, in which the subject as such "disappears." (*Zen and the Birds of Appetite,* pp. 23-24)

The dynamics of emptying and of transcendence accurately define the transformation of the Christian consciousness in Christ. It is a kenotic transformation, an emptying of all the contents of the ego consciousness to become a void in which the light of God or the glory of God, the full radiation of the infinite reality of His Being and Love are manifested. (Ibid., p. 75)

The only trace of distinction that remains between them [God and the soul] is the fact that what is God's by nature is the soul's by participation and by God's free gift. (*What Are These Wounds?* p. 14)

The charity that is poured forth in our hearts by the Holy Spirit brings us into an intimate experiential communion with Christ. (*No Man Is an Island,* p. 137)

A man cannot enter into the deepest center of himself and pass through the center into God unless he is able to pass entirely out of himself and empty himself and give himself to other people in the purity of a selfless love. (*New Seeds of Contemplation,* p. 64)

There are undoubtedly many other quotations that could be brought from the writings of Father Louis, but I would like to move on to another Spiritual Father.

ABHISHIKTANANDA (FATHER HENRI LE SAUX, O.S.B.)

A few years ago I took part in a very interesting symposium at Oxford University where Cistercian monks and nuns from around the world met with a group of Orthodox monks. At one point in the discussion the Cistercians were lamenting the fact that there were so few true Spiritual Fathers among the Latin Christians today. The Orthodox added that they suffered from a similar lack. Knowing the importance of the Spiritual Father in Orthodox monasticism, we asked them how they made up for this. One of their number, Bishop Antonie, a Romanian monk, replied that they had to turn to the writings of the Fathers of the past. These holy men, alive in the Lord, could still engender spiritual sons and daughters through their holy, life-giving words. I think this is very true. And I think Fr. Henri Le Saux, the holy French monk, who lived for so many years as an Indian sannyasi, dying in December 1973, has left us such life-giving words in his little book entitled simply *Prayer* (Westminster Press). I would like to offer a number of quotations from this powerful little book which express well the inner reality of that contemplative practice which we have been calling centering prayer.

Entrance into prayer is an act of faith. Praying is simply believing that we are in the mystery of

God, that we are encompassed by that mystery, that we are really plunged into and immersed in it – "in him we live and move and have our being" (Acts 17:28) – that the mystery of God in its fullness is both inside and outside us, within and without, like the air which surrounds us and penetrates into the tiniest hollows of our lungs. (p. 6)

Faith, in short, is the coming face-to-face of man with God, the awareness of the divine Presence. Now, when we speak of this awareness we do not at all mean any kind of sensible or psychological awareness, in the manner, for instance, in which we are aware of the sun, or of the heat or light which come from it, or even of the mental processes which are at work in our minds during our waking hours. The awareness of faith is something both more real and much deeper. It takes place at the very center of our awareness of ourselves, behind and beyond everything of which we are or might be conscious. (p. 8)

The aim of prayer, indeed, is not to think about God, not to form conceptions of God, however strong and lofty they may be. It is for God Himself, for God beyond any sign and any veil, that the soul, fed by the Gospel and the Spirit, is thirsty. (p. 35ff.)

Yet is it not a fact that no image or idea which we may form of God is God Himself, but remains inevitably and forever simply what we think of God? . . . They are signs pointing to the Reality they represent, but they are forever unable to comprehend that reality, which stands in its aloneness far beyond the reach of any conception or imagination of man. (p. 34)

If God is hidden, it is because he is out of the reach of our senses or imagination, even of our mental perceptions . . . It is true that our reason can get at least some glimpse of his existence, and we learn even more about him through the revealed Scripture; yet he remains always beyond any conceptual knowledge that man can have of him. (p. 9)

The man who has made his abode in this centre of himself is by that very fact established at the very source and origin of God's self-manifestation. (p. 29)

The underlying idea is evidently that we must never be contented with living, even less with praying to and meeting God, on the surface of our being, at the level merely of our senses and minds. The real place of the divine Encounter is in the very centre of our being, the place of our origin, from which all that we are is constantly welling up. (p. 54)

Man is made not merely to work with his hands and to think with his mind, but also to adore in the deep silence of his heart. Even more than to adore, he is called to plunge into that silence and to lose himself there, unable to utter any word, not even a word of adoration or of praise; for no word can express the mystery of God, the mystery of man in the presence of God, the mystery of the Son in the eternal presence of the

Father. There the mind cannot even think or conceive a thought . . . (pp. 28, 29)

Indeed, since man is so constituted that without special discipline his efforts in any sphere are rarely fruitful, it is highly beneficial to set aside certain times, certain days or hours of the day, when he may be free from all other occupations, including vocal prayer and common worship. At such times he may devote himself with whole and undivided attention to the Presence, contented simply *to be,* his eyes turned inward, his ears attuned to the inner silence, aware only that *God is.* (p. 21)

But this at least can be asserted for all devout souls, that, as long as they continue to think or feel in prayer, they are still outside the Spiritual Centre. They should never be satisfied by any wonderful thought or any marvelous sense of peace or bliss they may experience. God is beyond. (p. 42)

Needless to say, I would highly recommend the reading of the whole of this excellent little book, which expresses the mature teaching of a wise and holy Spiritual Father.

FATHER ADRIAN VAN KAAM, c.s.sp.

I would like to add just a quote or two from another Spiritual Master, one still living, Fr. Adrian Van Kaam, a Dutch priest who has founded and directs the Institute of Man at Duquesne University. He has published many spiritual works. These quotes are taken from *On Being Yourself.*

Originality in the realm of the spirit is a losing
of myself in the Origin of all that is, in the
Ground of my being, in God. In losing myself I
find my true self at its very Center. I return as it
were to the Origin of all origins. I experience
everything as welling up from that Ground, my
unique self included . . . I am most near to and
most identified with the Eternal Origin that
makes me be in a unique way and calls me forth
as nothing else is called forth in this cosmos . . .
Spirituality in the most profound sense resides
in the core of my being, in my deepest self or
spirit. (pp. 53-54)

I find in my deepest self the mystery of my own
Origin, which is the Origin of all that is. In these
depths I feel at-one with God. I feel also at-one
with every person and thing that emerges from
the same Divine Ground. On the deepest level
of my life, it is no longer possible to distinguish
a vertical relationship to God and a horizontal
relationship to man. I can no longer see one
without at least implicitly experiencing the
other. (p. 25)

Father Van Kaam is here directing our attention
to a fruit of centering prayer, which is especially
important to the Christian in the daily living out of
his vocation. Through this prayer we come to sense
our real oneness with all in Christ, our God. Out of
this grows up a very real compassion, a feeling-with,
which enlivens our love, patience, kindness, and
longsuffering.

FROM EASTERN CHRISTIANITY

Before concluding I would like to add an indication of Eastern Christian sharing in this understanding of contemplative prayer. In the epilogue of his recently-published study of Saint Symeon, the New Theologian, *The Mystic of Light,* Father George Maloney writes:

> Because Symeon is speaking out of his own experience and relying much for confirmation on the writings of the early Fathers, he is describing a very delicate process of interior growth. He basically is showing how a Christian moves from a superficial, externally motivated relationship to God into a deeper person-to-person relationship. This process is one of moving farther and farther away from experiencing God through ideas and images found in the consciously thinking mind of man towards an immediate, intuitive experience of God, "face to face," as it were. The inner presence of the Trinity, like a magnet, draws man's "conscious attention" away from old mental concepts that have become worn out and lifeless into a new manner of intuitively experiencing or knowing God. (p. 210ff.)

The Exarch of the Russian Patriarch in London, Bishop Anthony Bloom, whose many writings on prayer have greatly enriched us in recent years, in his book *Beginning to Pray* tells us that it is a journey "not . . . into my own inwardness, but a journey through my own self, in order to emerge from the deepest level of self into the place where He is, the point at which God and I meet." It is, for the Bishop, a simple process of "knocking at the door and the attempt to go inside, to become an intimate of Paradise, of the place where prayer is possible . . . a door opens in the center of our being, and we seem to fall through it into the immense depths which, although they are infinite, are all accessible to us; all eternity seems to have become ours in this one placid and breathless contact." I do not need to point out the similarity here to the thought of Thomas Merton.

FOUR

Centering Prayer and TM

FREQUENTLY, IN THE COURSE OF A WORKSHOP OR retreat in which centering prayer is being taught, a participant will ask what is the difference between what he or she is being taught and TM (transcendental meditation). Such a question will usually come from one who has heard about TM through the media or from friends, perhaps has read about it, and, in some cases, has attended an introductory lecture; not from one who has actually been initiated into TM and has practiced it. These latter usually spontaneously note the differences between what TM has meant for them and their new experience in centering prayer.

This is not surprising. For there are some superficial similarities between the simple method of contemplative prayer we derive from *The Cloud of Unknowing* and the technique of TM. A person who has only superficial contact with one or the other of the two or both of them will note the similarities. But one who has a real knowledge of them both will readily perceive the essential difference.

I mentioned above how a TM initiator responded to a description of centering prayer: "Why, that's

TM." Certainly he knew TM deeply, but he had only a brief descriptive knowledge of the prayer. And thus he saw the superficial likenesses without the essential differences. The differences lie in part in the activity of faith, so it will always be difficult for one without Christian faith to perceive them.

It is not surprising for me to find similarities in these methods. As Fr. Adrian Van Kaam has said: "Spirituality implies certain structures, dynamics and laws of development. These are basically the same for all men no matter to what culture or religion they belong. There is a fundamental human spirituality. This basic spirituality becomes specified in accordance with the culture or religion in which a person lives" (*On Being Yourself*, p. 54).

At a certain stage in the practice of the Jesus Prayer, as it comes down to us in the Eastern Christian tradition from the fourth-century monks of Egypt through Saint Gregory of Sinai in the fourteenth century – the century of *The Cloud* – we find the method very similar to that of TM. I do not know the origins of the precise technique of TM, whether it originates with Guru Dev – Mahesh Yogi's master – in this century or whether he is simply handing on something precisely formulated by an older tradition. In any case, I doubt that there is any direct interdependence between it and the Christian traditional methods. What seems evident to me is that we can expect similar methods or techniques to arise in the various traditions, given that they are all concerned with the same human creature and his basic call to transcendence.

In making a comparison between centering prayer and TM I do not want to downgrade in any way the latter technique. I have seen too many derive very real benefits from it to do that. I believe a Christian can make use of the basic TM technique without any hesitation, and if he puts it into the context of faith (without in any way modifying the technique in itself) it can be for him an authentic method of contemplative prayer.

But let me point out the differences I see between the two methods. First of all on the more superficial level:

TM is more rigid. In an effort to preserve the purity of teaching, very precise and inflexible instructions are given in regard to the amount of time to be taken going into the meditation, during the meditation and coming out of it. The author of *The Cloud* knows no such rigidity. This is not only a consequence of the absence of watches in the fourteenth century. Medievals had methods for computing segments of time with considerable precision when they wished. Rather this flows from the whole subordination of the practice to the Holy Spirit, ever present and guiding the movement of the prayer.

In TM each is initiated personally and given a specially chosen meaningless sound to use in his meditation. Centering prayer can easily be taught to groups and each one chooses his or her own prayer word, one that does have meaning for the user.

TM must be taught by an initiator who has received rather extensive training under Mahesh Yogi's personal guidance. A special secret knowledge is necessary, but there are no moral prerequisites. The initiator may be leading what Christians and devout Hindus would consider a promiscuous life. To teach centering prayer, no special training is necessary. In fact, everyone who learns it is urged to pass it on to others. But it is a thing of faith and love. Only one who is truly seeking God in love – and this presupposes trying to live a good moral life: "He who loves Me, keeps My commandments" – can really learn this way of prayer.

There is a deeper, more significant difference within the methods themselves. The actual TM experience, with its meaningless sound, has no intentionality within itself. The goal aimed at is not in the actual practice. Indeed, the meditation itself might be rough, with the release of much stress. But the aim is being achieved – the purification of the nervous system for greater quality of life.

On the other hand, centering prayer expresses in itself the goal of the practice and, indeed, of man's whole life – union and communion with God. It is not primarily oriented to something else, even though it does in fact have far-reaching effects in the life of the meditator. I think Abhishiktananda expresses this well:

> It is the greatest mistake to suppose that moments devoted to silent prayer are merely a preparation for our work. Meditation, for instance, is not intended to make us capable of worthily fulfilling our duties of study, work, or social intercourse, nor even to assist our progress in humility or any other virtue. Contemplation is worth while in itself. It needs no further justification. No doubt such high times of prayer will cast their rays on the whole of life,

but this radiation will not be deliberately intended. It will happen quite spontaneously, as naturally as the diffusion of the rays of the sun, which spread light, warmth and life over the whole surface of the earth. (*Prayer*, p. 25)

Because of these differences, a Christian TM initiator who knows the two methods well has told me he thinks they are both necessary for the full development of Christian life. As he sees it, TM brings about the transformation of consciousness, while the prayer of *The Cloud* cultivates the heart. I appreciate the insight expressed here and accept in part the distinction being made. I can certainly agree that centering prayer is essentially an exercise of the heart, of love. But I do not know if one can exclude from its effects the transformation of consciousness. Thomas Merton often spoke of this, its importance and necessity. Yet he did not know anything about TM as such. He saw it being brought about through contemplative prayer. He was certainly familiar with *The Cloud of Unknowing* and the whole tradition and milieu out of which it comes.

However, it should be noted that while numerous scientific tests have established some of the physiological effects of TM, so far as I know, no such tests have been done with centering prayer. Those practicing the prayer do report some similarity of experience, yet subtle physiological and neurological effects can only be established by testing. Whether such testing will ever be undertaken I do not know. I rather doubt it, for as I have indicated, the prayer is more concerned with the immediate response to God than with its effects on the person praying.

FIVE

TM and Christian Prayer

MAHARISHI MAHESH YOGI INSISTS RATHER STRONGLY
that TM is not something that belongs to a particular
religion. And he is right. It is, as he says, a very
simple, natural technique. The Maharishi has received it from an ancient tradition, but as it is taught
it is by and large divorced from the Vedic back-
ground and philosophy. I say "by and large" because
Mahesh Yogi himself remains a Hindu monk, and as
he hands on the technique he tries to hand on also a
certain respect for the venerable tradition out of
which it comes. This in itself is good – the basic
human virtue of *pietas,* of gratitude. But the technique can stand on its own.

Mahesh Yogi is an admirable man – in many ways
a good example for the Christian apostle. He lived
many years in retirement as the disciple of "Guru
Dev" (Swami Bramananda Saraswati), becoming a
truly spiritual man. We in the West tend to want to
do too much too soon and end up doing a lot less.
Our novitiates and seminaries have, in all too many
cases, capitulated almost entirely to activism and
secularism, allowing little time or opportunity, not

to speak of practical instruction, for spiritual deepening.

Mahesh Yogi received a beautiful thing from Guru Dev and the ancient tradition. He was convinced that if he could get all men and women to begin meditating, to spend time twice daily going to their deeper selves and beyond that to the Absolute, mankind would come into an era of peace and collaboration that would lead to prosperity. And so, with little if any of this world's means, he set out from India to bring this way of peace to all.

Simple as a dove, but wise as a serpent, he knew the place to go was America. The people to get to were the upper middle class – they have the power in government, the money, the influence that could support a rapid expansion program. And it has. Now, fifteen years later, there are several international universities, TV networks, and thousands of centers bringing into realization a "world plan." TM has been taught in public school systems and Catholic schools, grade schools, high schools, colleges and universities, and special schools for prisoners, ethnic groups, adults, etc. It has even been taught in the United States Military Academy at West Point and in some Trappist monasteries.

The Maharishi is truly a spiritual man, and his aim, the aim of meditation, is the enlivening of the whole man. But as a wise teacher his first appeal to the scientific and materialistic American has been through a battery of scientific reports that demonstrate what TM does for one's physical and mental health, how it tones up mind and body. Not far behind, however, is teaching of this as a path to true human happiness found in a clean life, heightened respect for self and others, consideration, love, and peace. Mahesh Yogi reaches out to men and women where they are and leads them gently toward where he is.

And he is there. That is another important point. He is a living proof that what he teaches works. Perhaps nothing so undermines the Gospel message as the lives of some of us who have committed ourselves to delivering it. It is hard for a hearer to take its promises seriously when he sees the teacher of this way of life leading a very different kind of life, one marked more by the hierarchy of values of a materialistic world, when he looks in vain for an example of how this way does really lead to life. We can certainly profit from the example of the Maharishi's zeal as a teacher, but what can we do with what he teaches?

TM is a very simple technique. It takes a properly trained initiator only a few minutes to teach it to anyone. A sound mantra (a sound that has no meaning associated with it) is used to transcend effortlessly the ordinary states of waking, sleeping, dreaming, to enter a fourth state of consciousness: simple awareness. One descends into his deepest self and comes into the Absolute, leaving behind all that is relative. There is great peace, joy, rest here, for one is finding his or her truest self, what he or she is all about.

My concern here is not with the many natural advantages that flow from this practice. They are many, and very real for the Christian, just as for any other man or woman. To plunge into deep, deep rest for fifteen or twenty minutes twice a day and to come out with renewed energy and clarity for the daily task is something very good indeed. But I want to take a look at what this experience is for the Christian operating with the insight of faith.

Mahesh Yogi, employing the terminology of the ancient Vedic tradition, speaks of this as experiencing the Absolute. The Christian knows by faith that this Absolute is our God of love, Father, Son, and Holy Spirit, who dwells in us. When he goes to his deepest self he finds himself, an image and participation of God, and he finds God Himself. But it is now not an objective experience but a wholly subjective one, an identification of two subjects leading to a unity of life and action.

This is one of the precious challenges the East is offering to us today. In the West we have come to think too exclusively in a subject-object context. We see ourselves related to God as an object out there, up there, in here. The East rather sees us and all creation as united to God, one with God. Without the sure guidance of revelation this sometimes comes out sounding like pantheism, and it sometimes is. But our oneness with God is a part of the Christian revelation too. "One is good, God." Anything that we are: goodness, truth, beauty, being, is of God, is a participation of God's goodness, truth, beauty, being – whatever that means. We will spend all eternity discovering it – the wonder of our being. In addition, the Christian has been baptized into Christ. "I live, now not I, but Christ lives in me." In some very real way we are identified with Christ, truly one with Him. Our Lord has said, "Whatever you do to

the least of these my brethren, you do to me." We
tend to understand Him as saying, "I will take it as
done to me." But that is not what He said. He proclaims an identity, a oneness of subject.

When we transcend by means of the TM technique, we come into an immediate experience of the
Absolute, of our God, an awareness of our oneness
with Him. We are not now contacting Him medi-
ately, through objects. We experience our oneness
with Him.

So far as I know, Thomas Merton never had any
contact with Maharishi Mahesh Yogi or with his
technique of transcendental meditation, yet he expresses these same ideas with great clarity and con-
ciseness in a number of places in his writings. Let me
quote again a couple of passages from his writings
that are relative to this:

> Unless we discover this deep self, which is hid-
> den with Christ in God, we will never really
> know ourselves as persons. Nor will we know
> God. For it is by the door of this deep self that
> we enter into spiritual knowledge of God. (And,
> indeed, if we seek our true selves it is not in
> order to contemplate ourselves but to pass be-
> yond ourselves and find Him.) (*The New Man*, p.
> 32)

> It starts, not from the thinking and self-aware
> subject, but from Being, ontologically seen to be
> beyond and prior to the subject-object division.
> Underlying the subjective experience of the in-
> dividual self there is an immediate experience
> of Being. This is totally different from an expe-
> rience of self-consciousness. But it is completely

non-objective. It has in it none of the split and alienation that occur when the subject becomes aware of itself as a quasi-object. The consciousness of Being . . . is an immediate experience that goes beyond reflexive awareness. It is not "consciousness of" but *pure consciousness*, in which the subject as such "disappears." (*Zen and the Birds of Appetite*, pp. 23-24)

The italics are Merton's own, and this is precisely what Mahesh Yogi underlines. This fourth state of consciousness is a state of pure consciousness. The man lacking faith can indeed have this experience of God. He may or may not recognize God in the experience. His motives for seeking this experience can be many and varied and the benefits derived also quite varied.

But the Christian who takes up TM, if his vision and motivation are enlivened by his faith, realizes by this faith that he is entering upon a way of very pure prayer. He is leaving all behind, all his thoughts, feelings, desires, in order to enter into God. Even if in a particular instance he does not actually transcend and enter into the fourth state of consciousness, his motivation, his outreach toward God is still there as very real prayer. And the quieting and rest prepare him well to enter at the end of his fifteen or twenty minutes of TM into more traditional forms of affective or meditative prayer. If he does transcend, and this will commonly be the case, he enters into a very restful and beautiful state of contemplation, of contemplative union with God.

In transcendental meditation a natural method is employed. It is different from classical Christian meditation that the authors commonly describe as leading to acquired contemplation, but as we have seen, it is not without parallels in our tradition. With TM or with these other methods of meditation, it is the motivation, insight, and outreach that come from a grace-activated faith that make the meditation true prayer. It is not the activity of unaided human nature, but a movement motivated and illumined by faith that makes TM Christian prayer. And this faith must be constantly nourished by contact with the Word, through daily reading of the Scriptures and frequent reception of the Eucharist. The TM technique in itself is not changed, but the resulting experience is a much more complete one, responding to all the levels of being in the divinized and Christed person.

A hesitation a Christian might have about reaching God through TM is that it seems to leave out the Cross, the death-resurrection experience that is at the heart of Christianity. Traditional ways of prayer and spiritual growth call for a long program of self-purification, of dying to self. TM seems to plunge right into God.

Perhaps in this it is actually more Christian than some of our traditional programming. Jesus did say simply, "Come to me, you who are burdened." He did not stipulate that we must first get rid of our burdens of sin and misery and be well bathed in virtue. In TM one seeks the immediate experience of God and seeks it in the most significant way – by doing something concrete to get it. And God, good to His word, "Seek and you shall find," is not slow in responding.

But the essence of the death-resurrection experience, of dying to self – that false superficial self, not the true self in Christ-God – is not lacking in TM. In fact it is very present. Already in the fidelity of stopping twice a day and making time for the meditation there is some very real asceticism. For not a few moderns it certainly is a difficult thing to do – to stop doing and be. But in the very practice itself there is a very real dying to self. As the mind settles down and the attention goes beyond all thought, as the meditation transcends and enters into pure consciousness, the meditator leaves behind all his beautiful (and not so beautiful) thoughts, feelings, imaginings – all that comes from himself. This is indeed dying to self. But in TM one does not dwell on this because it is so centered on the goal. And maybe this is one of the very real failures of some of our more complicated traditional ways – they have developed so fully that much attention is focused on the way – the dying – and the goal is all but lost sight of. The cross without the resurrection has absolutely *no* meaning. Maybe here is another lesson for us. Are we Christians sufficiently aware of, do we sufficiently proclaim the risen life that is already – even now – ours in Christ?

TM is a very simple, natural technique that enables a person to enter into the deepest self and find there the Absolute. For the Christian who undertakes it to find God it is pure prayer and faith tells us the Absolute we experience in the depths when we transcend the ordinary states of consciousness is our God of love, Father, Son, and Holy Spirit.

This immediate experience of God, which the TM technique has facilitated by pushing aside as it were all the concepts and images that are usually in the way, is beyond all concepts and images, all words and media of human expression. That is why we cannot express it adequately. We know the experience, but when we come out of it we are at a loss to say exactly what happened. But the ensuing peace, joy, benignity – the fruits of the Spirit – are a validation of its reality – "You judge a tree by its fruits."

But gradually the experience of God will begin to overflow the time spent in meditation. It will abide with us as we return to the affairs of the relative world. The Maharishi speaks of this as cosmic consciousness – when one remains in the absolute even as he attends to the relative. Saint Teresa of Avila drew a more graphic picture of it. She said her life flowed along constantly as two great rivers – one plunging wholly into God, the other flowing with the multitude of practical daily details that filled her days and nights. But the two rivers are really one.

The idea of an abiding presence of God is certainly not absent from Christian thought – it is most present. We have understood the Gifts of Wisdom, Knowledge, and Understanding as the Divine Presence active in us, enabling us to see and understand even as He does. This corresponds to what Mahesh Yogi calls the sixth state of consciousness. Formerly he called it God consciousness, but of late he more frequently refers to it as "gc" or glorified cosmic consciousness. It is when in all the relative things manifest to us we perceive also the unmanifest Ab-

solute; in the created we see the presence of the
Creator.

The seventh and highest state of consciousness
for Mahesh Yogi is unity of consciousness. There are
various nuances within this state, but essentially it
is the realization that the Absolute we perceive in
everything else is the same Absolute in myself and
that all are one in the Absolute. One of the effects of
Mystical Marriage, as it is described by the classical
Christian authors, is that one experiences that all that
is one's is God's and all that is God's is one's own.
"That they might be one, Father, even as we are one,
I in them and you in me, that they might be perfectly
one."

The way, then, traced out by the Maharishi, to be
attained by the regular practice of TM, corresponds,
step by step, to classical Christian teaching. His aim,
through the experience of unity in the Absolute, is
clarity of vision, universal love, and compassion – a
"feeling with" all creation. Rightly then is Mahesh
Yogi convinced that if all men embarked on this way
and faithfully pursued it, it would lead to an era of
universal peace.

Christians have always known (at least in theory)
that the Prince of Peace has come "to give light to
those who live in darkness and the shadow of death
and to guide their feet into the way of peace." And
He has said quite simply: "I am the Way." It is by
coming into conscious union with Him in the experience of deep prayer (whether by TM or any other
technique) that we enter into the Way of Peace.

SIX

Prayer and Liberation

THERE HAS BEEN A TENDENCY FOR MOST CHRISTIANS to dichotomize prayer and action, sometimes glossing over the separation by the old adage: to work is to pray. But one quickly discovers men and women who are both deeply concerned Christians of action and persons who are profoundly convinced of the role of prayer in that concerned action. I believe it is generally true that Christian activists are sensing more and more the importance of prayer in the movement toward liberation. But oftentimes they are unable to find any satisfactory articulation of this growing feeling. The contribution offered here will hopefully give them something with which to work.

That the world, our world, is in something of a mess at the moment, there can be little argument. There may be little all men and women can agree on, but on this they do, differing in opinion only as to how bad the mess is. More than a quarter of the globe's inhabitants profess to be Christians, disciples of Jesus Christ. It is, then, significant to find out what is the Christian response to this tragic situation. If God did indeed create us to share his life and happiness, if Christ's mission is one of recreation, renewal, even unto a new fullness, then how is this going to come about? How is life and order and a Garden of Eden going to rise again out of chaos? What is the Christian response to the chosen off-spring of Divine creative love whose very existence, not to speak of his full development, seems to be increasingly obstructed by all sorts of manipulation, by an unreasoned or misguided use of power, and even by brutal force? Or is there a Christian re-sponse?

Christ Himself is the response.

Christianity is following Christ, listening to Christ, *being* Christ. "Let this mind – this heart, this soul, this Spirit – be in you which was in Christ Jesus."

Christ Jesus was wholly free from interior op-pression. And so shall the Christian be, if he takes on the mind of Christ, if he lives what he has become by Baptism, if he allows his Christ-nature to breathe, to expand, to catch up his whole being in the move-ment of Love for the Father, which is Holy Spirit.

Jesus did know and experience exterior oppres-sion. We might even be tempted to say: in the end it killed Him. But that is the point, in the end though it had killed Him, He triumphed over it and lives. What was His response to the oppressive situation, His way to freedom? Union, communion with the Father, a communion that necessarily included obe-dience, for there can be union with the Father on no other terms: "Yes – Amen." Jesus' response to op-pression is prayer, communion with the Father and all that flows from it. And this is the Christian's response to all the oppression that rises out of the world's chaos, and to that chaos itself. For prayer is liberating, and the truly liberated man lives prayer.

To understand this we need to understand the two terms of our chapter title: "prayer" and "liberation."

The penny catechism – if there is anyone who can remember back to those far-off times when a penny could actually buy something, even a whole booklet – defined prayer for us as "lifting up the mind and heart to God." This is, of course, very figurative. God is not "up" or "down," nor in any other direction for that matter. Nor is the "heart" the sort of thing one starts "lifting up." Prayer is, rather, a happening. Or, better, a being present to. With the knowledge that comes from faith and the desire that is love, the Christian attends to the reality: God, actively present to him in the effectiveness of His creative love.

God does not just make things and then toss them out and let them be. Everything, in all its being and activity, is at every moment coming forth from, being sustained by and, indeed, participating in the goodness of the Divine Being.

This is true of all created being, of all that I perceive about me. Yet when it comes to the human person, the one who has been baptized into Christ, I find something even more wonderful. Not only does this particular Feature participate in the Divine Being *ab extrinseco*, from the outside, as it were. He certainly does that, like every other creature. Indeed, he does it most fully, being made to the image and likeness, able to know and to love – a creature radically free. But as one baptized, he has been brought into the very inner life and being of the Godhead.

Christians are sons and daughters of the Book. God, in His awful goodness – and it is something to inspire awe – has revealed to them His own inner life, His personal relationships. And in Baptism, He, Father, Son, and Holy Spirit, taking up His abode in them in a very special way, brings them into union with the Son. Sonship is the Christian's, not by some merely extrinsic legal fiction, but by some kind of intrinsic participation. "I live, now not I, but Christ lives in me."

This prayer is not going "up" or "out," nor even really "in." But it is a "being present to" the reality of what is here, and what one is. *Here* is God, in His creative goodness, at this very moment and at every moment, bringing one forth into existence, sharing with one His being. *What* one is is a creature whose whole being is constantly receptively in contact with God, coming forth from Him, and wholly oriented to Him as end and meaning – the One Who alone can fulfill the thirsting capacities to know and love that He has created in His creature. Even more, the baptized is, in some most wonderful way, Christ, the Son, coming forth from the Father, and returning to Him in the personal response of love that is the Holy Spirit. Of its very nature His whole being is to the Father. The Spirit cries out, in groans that lace every fiber of His being together in an ardent movement of love: "Abba, Father." *This is the reality of His being.* And prayer is only letting it be. One simply stops distracting oneself from this movement of love that He actually is.

Thus prayer is, in its essence, liberation – making the self free to be what it really is. When I enter into prayer and simply let myself be, I then enjoy the freedom of the Son of God. Interiorly Jesus could be subject to no form of oppression – there He was essentially free. So, too, is the Christian when, in prayer, we come into our deepest self and simply are what we are, one with God in a deepest union of subjects. At this level of being nothing can ever enslave; we are radically free. Apart from those impairments of human nature that render us functionally something less than human, the human person remains forever free. Once we have received the precious gift of divine filiation, only we can renounce it, and that we must do freely, taking on the slavery of sin.

Passion, psychological pressures, the construct of a false identity, while these cannot take away that radical freedom or the basic orientation toward God, they can limit and impede its use and enjoyment. This is a form of oppression and calls for liberation. The imperious demands of the loins and the pocketbook – of lust and greed – can really enslave. But it is easy to free oneself from these compared to the socioeconomic shackles that bind with demands to keep up with the Joneses and indeed to outdo them. The shackles of our Americanism, our professionalism, our class, are made of weightier metal. We need to free ourselves, our true self, our deepest self, from the false, superficial self that is created and shaped and in the end totally dictated by these extrinsic forces. But how can we escape them? Go off to a monastery? That is a solution few can embrace – and even the monastery is in many ways, willy-nilly, involved in the society and economy that surrounds it and in part sustains it. The commune in the woods is even less of a solution.

The Christian response is mortification, dying to self, the superficial, controlled self, so that the true self can live in the light of Truth. Know the Truth and the Truth will make you free.

But how does one die? Something of it is found even in the very knowledge that one needs to die, but does not know how to. It is at best a slow process. If you would find the Way, the Way that is the freeing Truth – "be my disciple, take up your cross daily and follow me." It is much in the pain of dying and not being able to die. Christ hung on the Cross three eternal hours. It is a long, slow process, and prayer is at the heart of it; daily prayer, which reveals the freeing Truth, gains the needed help, gives the motivation.

We will not go on praying if we do not find something in prayer. But we do find something there – that Truth whose searching light brings forth with unescapable clarity the truth of all other things. We then see how false are the claims of so much of the social mores and Madison Avenue brainwashing that have been fabricating the meaning of our lives. We see true values, so we can let go of many of the mirages, and we can use the good things of creation as if we used them not. Christ loved the poor with a special love, but he did not preach poverty – rather, poverty of spirit, the freedom to get along with and without. In prayer human relations come alive – in the depths of our being we find unity, unity with God in Christ and every other human – and we want to be with – with people. The rest – all the wonderful trinkets of creation – become so much more precious when they are shared, and undesirable when they are had at the cost of sharing.

Prayer and the call to sharing do not necessarily require us to go out from our land and our people, from our class and our station in life. (I almost said, from our parents' people – but in fact in so many cases in America, the upper middle class are the children of immigrants and have fought their way up. They have gone out from their parents' people and it is perhaps hardest for these to identify with their shadows, and seek and accept solidarity with those whom they have left behind or those who have come later to fill the ghettos they have eagerly abandoned.) But they may. They have sent men and women to the crumbling inners of Chicago and many other cities to share what they have and what they are. They have called a professor friend of mine to sell his piece of suburbia to buy an apartment house in the neighborhood from which he emerged and to fill it with an extended family of students and elderly. But we might stay with our class, might even stay in suburbia. But our values will necessarily change. We will be ashamed of some of the things our class stands for, some of the pseudo-values it selfishly exalts. Our lifestyle will change. And with the critical and creative insight that emerges from contact with Truth, we will seek and find new ways.

I think here of Packard Manse, an ecumenical community in the Boston suburbs. It is a cluster of family units that includes also a monastic unit where two monks go about their prayerful thing, fulfilling the prophetic and priestly role that no community can afford to be without. The houses and setting are typical suburbia, though the large interracial families tell of a difference. But through co-ops, extended hospitality, conscientization, this community is freeing itself from many of the conforming pressures of its class and environs, and indeed invites those environs to share in its freedom.

But let us not think that it is only suburbia or the middle class or the "have's" that need to be liberated. Perhaps the "have not's" need it even more. For their very need can be the fertile seminary of enslaving greed. It is easier to tell the rich they are better off and must share, than to tell those in ghettos that they have twenty or fifty times more than their sisters and brothers in Bangladesh and so must open their grasping hands and give up one of the widow's two mites.

Prayer does not unite us with the rich or the poor, it unites us with humankind. Let me quote that most beautiful word of Thomas Kelly which sums up so well what God does to us in prayer:

He plucks the world out of our hearts,
    loosening the chains of attachment,
And he hurls the world into our hearts,
    where we and he together carry it in
        infinitely tender love.

A Testament of Devotion, p. 47

The kind of prayer we speak of here, essential prayer, is quite different from the kind of prayer that some might be most accustomed to: a constant litany of petitions. I do not want to downgrade, in any way, petitionary prayer. Jesus Himself taught it in that

most perfect prayer: Our Father, who art in heaven
. . . But prayer cannot end with petition. Nor should
it begin with it. Indeed, such prayer may be feeding
our greed and increasing our enslavement to our
needs, real or imaginary.

If prayer is communion, union, then we pray-ers
know in Whom we believe. And this knowledge
must break forth in praise and worship as we realize
Who that is. We are filled with joy, satisfaction and
pleasure at being able to communicate with Him, to
praise Him, to be one with Him. How this diminishes
needs, frees from false needs.

When we realize who God is and who we ourselves are, and the utter gratuity of all creation, a
total thanksgiving wells up from the very depths of
a grateful, receiving being. All is gift, and gratefully
received. Greed is gone. Nothing is taken for
granted. All is reverenced. "I thank you, God, for the
wonder of my being." Ecological well-being is the
necessary consequence. There is a loving care for
every person and every thing. Sufficiency is more
than enough, for it is more than is deserved. It is
what is wanted for all. And what one has is shared
with all, with that end in view.

At this point enter penitence, forgiveness, and
being forgiven, healing resentments, greed, selfish-
ness. These are freeing experiences we all very much
need. Even the oppressed can never be truly liberated until they forgive their oppressor.

But does the role of prayer end here: freeing the
individual pray-er and others insofar as they are
moved to share and to forgive? No.

There is a role of prayer in political thought, political passion, and political action. We do not want to deny the continuing validity of Paul's analogy of the Body. Not all are called to promote Christ's redemptive mission by political or social activism. Not all pray-ers are called to be social activists, even though all Christian activists must be pray-ers. But prayer addressed to and in contact with the authority of the power of God and enlivening one's bonds with all humankind increasingly stimulates, deepens, and enriches political thought and calls for supportive solidarity with those who are expressing Christ's healing presence on the political and social fronts.

And this support, this universal concern, can, and must, for the Christian who has entered into true prayer, express itself in the power of intercession. As we enter more freely into and realizes more fully our identity with Christ, all Christ's concerns become our concerns, even as all our concerns are Christ's. As we take on the mind of Christ, the one Mediator, we come to understand the meaningfulness of intercessory prayer. For we understand that even at the very moment as God is creating and re-creating, God hears our prayer. Christ said it would be so. It is something quite staggering to realize that the very God has so disposed that the unfolding of His creative sharing of His own infinite goodness, being, and joy should be shaped in some way by a human petitioner's good will or lack of it. But such is His will. And hence with compassion and sensitivity born of true love the Christian must constantly make intercession.

What does this realization not say of the Christian's true significance and dignity? Is this not a liberating realization: that God so esteems the human person. Need we then be unduly concerned about how our fellows value us? With all the creative power of God at our call – "ask and you shall receive" – need we fear any lack?

There are many, many more things that could be said here of prayer and liberation. We could see how prayer liberates in the face of every created power by placing it in the context of true power – God's. We could indicate how true prayer increases one's attentiveness, so that one is more constantly and fully in touch with reality; increases one's creativity, so that the real problems of life are perceived, new alternatives are seen, and ultimately God's answers are found; how prayer increases awareness of responsibility, so that one does not need to be coerced to do one's share; rather one humbles oneself for failures and seeks forgiveness through genuine conversion; and how prayer even increases relaxation, so that one can let go of more and more of defensive mechanisms and freely relate with fellow humans.

Prayer liberates. But it does far more than that. It revolutionizes. Ultimately in prayer one comes to understand the quintessence of Christian belief and practice:

> Blessed are the poor in spirit, for theirs is
>   the kingdom of heaven.
> Blessed are those who mourn, for they
>   shall be comforted.
> Blessed are the meek, for they shall
>   inherit the earth.

Blessed are those who hunger and thirst for
    righteousness, for they shall be satisfied.
Blessed are the merciful, for they shall
    obtain mercy.
Blessed are the pure in heart, for
    they shall see God.
Blessed are the peacemakers, for
    they shall be called sons of God.
Blessed are those who are persecuted
    for righteousness' sake, for
    theirs is the kingdom of heaven.

                                 Matt. 5:3-10

SEVEN

Faith Sharing

OUR FATHER ABRAHAM WAS A "WANDERING JEW." And so are we wanderers. A new Moses leads us through the desert of this world, where there are few good spiritual watering holes. But if we stay close to that Rock we will always be able to draw from the Fountain of Living Water. We are pilgrims, members of the Pilgrim People of God. We are on a return journey, going back to our Father's house.

It is true, like Cain, we have sinned. But happily we have not been condemned, like one accursed, to wander alone on the face of the earth. We have been incorporated into a people, a body. The Creator, when He first looked upon His creation, man, knowing him through and through, averred, "It is not good for man to be alone." And forthwith He gave him a helpmate like unto himself, to share his joys, and, in time, also his sorrows. They went forth, a pair, to begin their wandering on the face of the earth. And later, when the Redeemer promised to them came, He sent out His heralds, two by two, to show their descendants the way back.

There can be no doubt that in God's loving design, man is not meant to walk the arduous path of faith alone. "It is a narrow gate and a hard road that leads to life," and we all very much need the encouragement and support of another as we move along it, year after year, sometimes dragging our feet, often conscious of the ruts and rocks, the mud and mire, the good hidden beyond tortuous turns and arduous ascents.

For this reason most followers of Christ are invited to find a helpmate for the journey, either in the Sacrament of Matrimony or within a community of shared commitment. And yet, I am afraid it is a fact that the vast majority of Christians who vow to share the journey together find that on a day-to-day basis, while they freely share most of the other aspects of their lives, they rarely feel free to share in an articulate way their spiritual journey. What sharing there is is largely non-verbal, in that they worship and say prayers together, addressing their common Lord, and seek to keep His commandments and follow after Him, but rarely talk to each other about Him and their relationship to Him.

Happily this is not a universal pattern. With the renewal of Christian life, more and more Christians are coming to spontaneous shared prayer, where they express openly before those who are journeying with them the movements of their hearts to the Lord. More particularly, within the charismatic movement, and especially within charismatic households, a full sharing of the journey in the Lord has become the common practice. The members can count on their brothers and sisters to help them hear the Lord, discern His will and follow it with ever increasing fidelity. At shared prayer, which begins the day, ends the day and fills in many of the minutes in between, one's joys and sorrows, hopes and needs are the common concern as all together openly express their deep desire to move ahead steadfastly in the footsteps of the Lord as true disciples.

And yet there are not a few Christians, even among committed religious who have joined each other in community precisely to share this journey, who find the concept of shared prayer and any kind of intimate sharing of their journey in the Lord repugnant. From the training and formation they have received it seems somewhat like indecent exposure. This is a segment of their lives that is strictly private. At most it might be shared with a Spiritual Father or Mother, if one is fortunate enough to have one. To share even the good things the Lord is doing in their lives would be wrong. It could lead to pride and give others a false opinion about them.

This is a rather sad situation. I do not think those who see things this way are to be judged. By no means. It is the way things were, for better or for worse, when they were being formed in the way of Christian life. But it is sad.

SHARED PRAYER

Rosalind Rinker has a wonderful little book. It is called *Prayer: Conversation with God* (Zondervan). It is concerned largely with shared prayer. It is based on the word of Scripture: "I tell you solemnly once again, if two of you on earth agree to ask anything at all, it will be granted to you by my Father in heaven. For where two or three meet in my name, I shall be there with them." Her sixth chapter is entitled: "Why Pray Aloud Together?" In summary she gives five answers, well worth pondering:

- Because Jesus promised that when two of His disciples (that means us today) meet to pray, He will be there with them. Our risen, living Lord said and meant what He said: "I am there, right among them." In a particular way, in a particular promise, He is present.

- Because Jesus knows the problems of life press in upon us when we are alone until the spirit is almost broken, the mind refuses to accept reality, and so escapes into a world of its own. Burdens shared become lighter. "Bear one another's burdens," said Paul. Before I learned the secret of prayer together, I thought that my burdens were greater than anyone else's burdens. Now I know they aren't, and now I know a way to help instead of always wanting to be helped.

- Because as we pray the Spirit of our Lord has our attention. He is always conscious of us, but we need to focus our attention and our consciousness upon Him. Then He can whisper to us the love plans He has for us. Sometimes these directions come to two or more persons in the group at the same time. We find ourselves in total agreement in all that we are asking. This leaves no room for wavering, for double-mindedness or doubt. We have agreed in His presence and He gives us the agreement.

- When we pray together we become bold and honest, and ask for things we never intended asking for at all.

- Praying with other people gives us new sisters and new brothers in Christ. The more we pray with other people the more we begin to trust them, and the more honest we all can be about our personal needs. Selfconsciousness drops away and we can pray about our real problems, not just surface ones. Genuine "togetherness" is a God-given state, and hearts are joined in His presence.

  (Prayer: Conversation with God, pp. 44-45)

I do not think, though, that anyone who has had the experience of real shared prayer has any need of arguments to be convinced of its value and even necessity in the life of a Christian. A person need but once have an experience of the consolation, encouragement, and strengthening that come from having a loving friend pray at one's side in an hour of sorrow or desolation. But the first breakthrough is often difficult. We feel very awkward the first time we try to articulate a prayer of our own. And it certainly is a stepping out in faith to speak openly and personally to One Whose presence is perceived only by faith. If some without faith were to walk into the room, they would think we were crazy – or so we feel. As we invite others to share prayer with us, especially in groups, a great deal of sensitivity is called for. We have to love and embrace our brothers and sisters where they are and not demand that they measure up to our standards or conform to our ideas.

There is a very delightful story coming from the early days of the Shakers. The Shakers were a reform group from the Quakers. As one wag put it: when the Quakers stopped quaking, the Shakers started shaking. Vibrant enthusiasm marked their worship services. In the time of Father Joseph, the second leader of the reform, in the course of a very lively meeting, one of the sisters fell and broke her leg. Forthwith Father Joseph went off into retreat for six weeks. When he returned, he assembled the community and assured them that God did not take delight in disorder, and certainly did not want His children to be breaking legs. So he had spent the six weeks devising dance steps so they could express their enthusiasm in an orderly way. Most in the community were delighted and took to the dances with great spirit. But a few of the old-timers, who harked back to the days of Mother Anne, the foundress, sat stolidly on the side, not deigning to join in. After a bit Father Joseph came over to them. Gently he said to them, "I can appreciate how you find it difficult to go along with these new ways. But couldn't you, just to show your love and oneness, just wave your hand once in a while?"

We can welcome our reticent brothers and sisters to a shared prayer, assuring them their simple presence is supportive and meaningful to us. Perhaps they can occasionally say an "Amen" or an "Alleluia." It is good from time to time to say an "Our Father," a "Hail Mary" or a "Glory be," with which all can feel at ease in praying aloud. If our silent brothers and sisters are made to feel welcome, the day usually comes when a burden of the heart, a hope, a fear, a real need, leads them haltingly to articulate a first hesitant prayer. A warm, sensitive affirmation of such a prayer breaks down further hesitancies. And soon another comes personally to experience the many blessings of being able to share prayer.

I should note, in passing, that when I use the expression "shared prayer" to mean a spontaneous, personal sharing, I do not by any means want to indicate that this is the only kind of shared prayer there is. Whenever Christians pray together, we have shared prayer. But I am afraid that many of us have realized that, as we stand or sit together, reciting various prayer formulas, perhaps more often than we would care to admit, there is little real praying going on in us and little sense of being with our brothers and sisters in their prayer. When we pray aloud spontaneously, the words of necessity arise from prayer of the inner person. And as we hear our brother or sister articulate his or her prayer, we very consciously and personally respond to it and make it our own.

There is, of course, a whole spectrum of shared prayer, from the quiet sitting of the Quaker meeting with its occasional speaking out, to the Pentecostal gathering where the constant quiet murmur periodically erupts in a crescendo of enthusiastic praise. I know at our own abbey we experience the variety. The weekly prayer meeting of the brethren used to be more like a Quaker meeting than anything else. But since a number of novices have joined us who were active in large charismatic groups before their entrance into the monastery, our meetings have become much more vocal. And it is when we have an ecumenical Pentecostal group with us for a weekend retreat that our meetings really explode. As the waves of praise and prophecy surge on hour after hour, I sometimes cannot help but chuckle and say, "Lord, you must really be enjoying this, to be pouring out such a sustained spirit of enthusiasm!"

As we become Christians of more and more lively faith, our Lord's words: "Where two or three are gathered in my name there I am in the midst of them" become more meaningful to us. Whenever we come together with a fellow Christian, whether it be but a chance encounter on the street, a formal visit at home or office, sitting by the bed of a sick friend or enjoying an outing or a social event together, always our being together as Christians brings a Third Person there in a special way. To simply ignore this reality is sad. We are the losers. All these experiences can be enriched and made more beautiful and fruitful if we advert to His presence and consciously call upon Him to be a part of our sharing. What a difference it makes, when we are sitting at the bedside of a sick friend feeling very helpless to say or do anything really significant, to recall His powerful loving presence. At that point, to take up the Scriptures and hear some of His consoling words and then commit the whole need to Him have an effect something like opening the blinds and letting the warm morning sunlight flood into a room after a dark, cold night. How often is the whole climate of a meeting changed when the group or couple stops for a minute or two to turn to the Lord there present. Tenseness evaporates, new lights on the matter shine out, the sharers experience their oneness and common intent, new openness develops, a meeting that was perhaps at a standstill moves on toward a satisfying conclusion.

Again and again we experience this sort of thing.
Even the chance encounter on the sidewalk or at the
bus station can rise from being a banal social response to an uplifting moment of grace if the two or
three can exchange a word that evokes the faith
experience of a loving Presence.

We would think it downright impolite if, when
we encountered a friend, he completely ignored a
mutual friend who was at our side. Yet how often do
we ignore the Friend who is right there when we
meet. Is it that we do not believe – or just a shyness
in translating our faith into action?

At the conclusion of our workshops we usually
have a "sending" service where each receives a small
pocket edition of the New Testament. We encourage
the participants to carry the Good News with them
as much as possible, and in their sharings with fellow Christians not only to advert to the Lord's presence and speak to Him but to let Him speak, too, out
of His inspired and inspiring Word. The more we
can consciously bring our Lord into our lives, the
more we will live in the fullness of the joy of His
resurrection, into which we have been baptized.

WALKING TOGETHER

Our sharing as Christians must not end with shared
prayer, however fundamental and important that
might be. We need the Gospel sharing just mentioned. We need, in fact, to be able to share directly,
personally, intimately with some "fellow traveler"
every aspect of our journey in faith, all of its joys and

sorrows, successes and failures, its loneliness and its communality.

There is a terrible loneliness in sin and failure – until it is shared; then there is a real communion. One of the very beautiful moments in a human life occurs when one finally comes to the decision to share with another that deep dark truth that hides in his depths. We have felt, perhaps for years, that if others knew of it, it would be the end. We would no longer be loved or respected. But we cannot go on that way. We need to be accepted and loved for who we truly are, even with this dark spot. We finally blurt it out, and discover that it really does not change things at all. Or, more often, that this openness and sharing produces a deeper, fuller, richer bond of love and respect. And we know now we are fully accepted and loved for who we really are.

Some years ago, when the Jesuits were moving their theologate from St. Mary's in Kansas to St. Louis, they consulted the Menninger Behavioral Institute in Topeka on how they might best arrange their new quarters to foster Christian community. In the course of his response, Dr. Menninger noted that for people to relate well generally, they need to have in their life at least one or two intimate friends, a relatively small group of close acquaintances among whom they can be fully at ease and a larger group with whom they identify. In the case of the Jesuits and religious in general, the last might be their institute, the second, their local community or a subdivision of it, if it be large. Oftentimes it is the first that is neglected – the intimate friend. Such friendship cannot be structured, only fostered and encouraged.

This fostering should include the practical element of providing time and space for friendship. If the demands put on a life are such that there is no time left to be with friends regularly, friendship and intimacy simply cannot develop. And if there are not places and situations where two can be alone regularly, again intimacy cannot grow. This is as true in lay life as in religious community.

And I think all this is as true for the faith life as it is for human life as a whole. It seems to me significant that from the twelfth century, the century that was perhaps the most truly Christian century in the West, the century when – I believe for the only time – Western Christendom was guided by a single spiritual leader to whom Pope and king, emperor and common folk turned, we have many of our finest treatises on "spiritual friendship." Unfortunately, and for mostly wrong reasons, this significant dimension of Christian life suffered a severe eclipse. However, until fairly recently it was somewhat supplied by a regular father confessor or spiritual director. This was usually a one-way relationship rather than the full, mutual sharing of friends, but it at least gave one someone with whom to share the inner journey, someone who cared, prayed, offered understanding, counsel, and encouragement.

For a time, though, even this kind of sharing seemed to fall into the shadows. But now there are more and more Christians, religious and lay, seeking a spiritual director or Spiritual Father. As has always been the case, however, there seem to be relatively few qualified and willing to fulfill these roles. As a result, Christians have been turning more and more to one another, and spiritual friendship is reviving. This is very true in the charismatic communities. The French Canadians are speaking more broadly of *accompaniment spirituel*. We are learning to walk more openly with one another on the journey of faith and love.

There is a remarkable ecumenical church in Washington, D.C., called the Church of the Savior. It was started after the war by an ex-chaplain, Gordon Crosby. It calls for a very specific commitment on the part of the members. Each must truly strive after personal holiness and also take part in a particular mission of the parish, an outreach in faith to the larger community. As the parish grew from its original half dozen to its present 150, it became increasingly difficult, if not impossible, for the Reverend Crosby to respond to the needs of each for guidance in the faith journey. A couple of years ago one of the mission groups (they usually have about twelve members in the group) conceived of a plan whereby they would help each other. The members of the mission were paired off, to spend three months being special "faith-full" friends to each other. The partners met weekly to pray together, share Scripture and share their spiritual journey. They gave each other a sort of spiritual autobiography. Each three months the group rotated partners. In time all the members of the mission had a chance for this deep sharing in faith with every other member in the group. The experiences were uneven, but on the whole very positive. The courage involved was amply rewarded. The members generally found not only a lot of support and deepening of commitment to Christ and one another, but a new humility in the face of each other's true Christian spirit. Many new gifts and creative talents surfaced for the benefit of the whole community.

Such structuring, at first, may seem somewhat artificial, but perhaps we need the encouragement of some structure. The three months' rotation had its pros and cons, but was perhaps best for this particular group's experiment. What this experiment does invite us to is not so much imitation of a particular structure but the courage to do some creative experimenting in our own life situation to facilitate the growth of spiritual friendship.

In our workshops we divided the groups into pairs or triplets and encouraged these to share in depth the whole experience they were having during the workshop, leaving ample time for such sharing. On the whole it has been a good experience, though not always as fruitful as some desired. It has relieved the leaders of the workshops from having to carry the burden of so much of the personal counseling and sharing. And, in not a few cases, the partnerships have perdured and continue to be supportively active. In some cases, where circumstances did not favor the partnerships continuing outside the workshop, the experience encouraged the participants to take the necessary steps to develop such a friendship back home. The beginning and basis for this were usually sharing with a friend the religious experiences of the workshop.

"It is not good for man to be alone." Most of us would agree with that not only because it is the Word of God but because our own life, if we have the courage to listen to it, tells us the same. What we need, then, is the daring to take the steps necessary to see that we do not have to go it alone on the journey of faith. This means, for one thing, to affirm concretely the value of spiritual friendship and to make time for it. It also means, in most cases, an initial stepping out in faith to begin sharing at this level. We will almost always find, though, if we choose with a certain amount of discretion, that our initiative will receive a very positive response, and the one to whom we turn will be very happy to have this opening to begin to share life at a deeper level.

Our God, of immense love, has so ordained things that the glory He seeks in His creation is to be found most fully in the happiness of His beloved children. The journey in faith, which is to culminate in the sharing of the vision, is supposed to be a foretaste of its fullness of joy. The fruits of the Spirit – love, joy, peace – are meant to be tasted each day along with others. Patient suffering is one of them. The daily cross is a part of Christian discipleship. But, as the priest used to say in the marriage service, as he spoke to the couple of the sufferings they would have to share together: perfect love will make it a joy. When a hand-clasp is communicating to us the presence of a loving friend we can walk down any road, even through the valley of the shadow of darkness, the valley of dark faith, with joy, with confidence, with peace, with assurance. Happiness consists in knowing what we want, what our nature calls out for and our freedom chooses, and knowing we have it or are on the way to getting it. When we walk with another in faith, we know what we want and we know we are on the way.

EIGHT

Mary

The Faith-full Woman

ON THE LAST EVENING OF OUR WORKSHOPS I ALWAYS
like to have some sharing on Mary, the faith-full
woman, the delight of God's heart, the one about
whom we can quite literally say: The Greatest. And
yet the one so tender, so loving, so approachable.

Elizabeth said of her cousin, "Blessed is she who
has believed." But Mary's faith did not end with an
assenting nod; it was fully lived out in practice. As
her Son said, "Who is my mother? . . . The one who
does the will of my Father . . ."

How do we get to know this wonderful woman,
this model of Christian faith? We can really know
her only through faith. We get to know her as we get
to know her Son – by listening to the word of faith,
by dialogical reading, by meeting her regularly in
prayer.

At times I have heard it said that there is very
little about Mary in the Scriptures. I do not think this
is so. Loving Mary, of course, we would like to know
much more, know all, and penetrate deeply into the
unique beauty of this woman. But what we have is
certainly abundant, more than we can ever hope
fully to fathom. In a few pages of sharing I can only

hope to touch its surface, perhaps indicate a few doorways through which the reader can enter gardens of unequaled beauty, full of the fruits of the Spirit.

We are all quite used to hearing of seven words of Christ, those spoken from the Cross. But have you ever noticed the fact that we have seven words of Mary? Scripture records for us her utterances only seven times. Yet in these seven words there is a fullness of wisdom. In them we can find a complete rule of life, a way to live out our faith relation with God in a total manner.

"BUT HOW . . ."

As the Annunciation scene opens we find a startled young virgin: startled to hear of her dignity, startled to hear of her call. In the wonderful moment of faith awakening who is not startled? When it first comes upon us, whether in a sudden crash, a bolt of lightning, a mighty wind or the murmur of a gentle breeze, this new realization cuts right through all the previous constructs of our self-identity. "Me – the well-beloved of God? Me – a partaker of divinity, truly one with Christ, the Son? Me called to be perfect, even as the heavenly Father is perfect?" The only response we can make is that modeled for us by Mary: "But how can this be?" It is a stance we will be forced to return to again and again in moments of light and grace when the full implication of our sublime call rises to fuller consciousness, as faith develops and the gifts become more active, and our own personal, particular role in the divine plan of love is made known to us. When Saint Paul tried to express this, he had to fall back on Scripture: "Things no eye has seen and no ear has heard, things beyond the human mind, that God has prepared for those who love him."

In the face of the wonder of it we can, sadly, turn to disbelief, like old Zachariah: "How can I be sure of this?" Or like Sarah, we can laugh at it as so much nonsense, a pipe dream. "An unspiritual person – one who does not have the Holy Spirit – is one who does not accept anything of the Spirit of God: one sees it all as nonsense, it is beyond understanding, because it can only be understood by means of the Spirit." Or one might run from it – it is judged to be too demanding. "Let me just settle down to everyday life. That's enough for me."

But the response of faith can only be that of Mary: "How are you going to bring it about?" There are problems, there are difficulties; humanly speaking, there are even impossibilities. Of myself I can only be a sterile field. How can I become pregnant with divine life? From whence will come the life-giving seed so that Christ will be formed in me, so that I will truly be another Christ, a perfectly responsive child of God?

"LET WHAT YOU HAVE SAID BE DONE . . ."

The answer to our question can only be essentially that answer which Mary received: "The Holy Spirit will come upon you and the power of the Most High will cover you with its shadow."

Of ourselves, we have good reason to disbelieve, to fear, to run and hide. Who can live up to the vocation that is ours as Christians? But the power of God is ready to work in us. "Look, I am standing at the door, knocking. If one of you hears me and opens the door . . ." The Spirit of God is ready to form Christ in us, to form in us His mind and His heart. We have but to open, to respond the way Mary shows us.

Indeed, at this moment Mary could very humanly have been overwhelmed by fear. Not only was the call, the vocation to which she was being summoned, a thing sublime and demanding beyond compare. It was also, humanly speaking, rather terrifying. This young girl was being asked to become an unwed mother in a very closed society. The law – that holy and wholly present Law – would demand that she be stoned; at least, what else could its very fallible prosecutors conclude? And yet the faith-full one can only make one response: "I am the servant of the Lord, let what you have said be done to me."

Thus, and only thus, is unleashed the divine power to accomplish in and through us the "great things."

"WHEN THE VOICE OF YOUR GREETING . . ."

Mary's yes to God was so total that He formed in her, in very flesh and of her flesh, Christ the only Son, even as He made her to be the one of all creation to be most identified with Him. To the extent that we, too, say yes will the Father through the Spirit form His Son in us, form us into His Son.

But Mary did not rest on her newly acquired dignity. The Lord's message had indicated to her a need: "Your cousin Elizabeth has, in her old age, herself conceived a son . . ." One who is in truth "the servant of the Lord" is the servant of all who are the Lord's. With the fearlessness born of faith – even while knowing all the fears of the first hours of a first pregnancy– and impelled by love, the little girl from Nazareth sets out across the alien land of the Samaritans into the sophistication of suburbia to offer her humble service.

But see what happens: "As soon as Elizabeth heard Mary's greeting, the child leapt in her womb and Elizabeth was filled with the Holy Spirit." Mary had not come with any mind to fulfill an apostolic mission, to be the bearer of the Good News, of the living Word of God. She came but to render a humble human service, to do an act of kindness, to respond to a human need. Yet, her merest presence, her simple arrival, brought life and grace and the powerful presence of the Spirit.

And so it will be with us. If we but listen to the word and open ourselves in deep prayer, say our existential yes and let the Most High form Christ in us, then as we go about our daily task, doing our simple human duties, we will be bringing Christ, His life, His love, His Spirit to each one we greet. No one can give what he does not have. But having, it is given, even without our conscious effort or intent. For this is the Lord's doing – and it is wonderful in our sight.

"MY SOUL PROCLAIMS THE GREATNESS OF THE LORD . . ."

Mary was fully conscious of what had happened to her, in her. She rejoiced to see the Son of God in her already beginning. His saving mission, and beginning with her beloved cousin and her cousin's yet unborn child. What was Mary's reaction in the face of all this wonder, this greatness? Our rather shallow, somewhat pseudo-humility would be inclined to make some show of disclaiming the reality or of trying to sort of hide it, or hide behind it. Not so the perfectly humble Virgin.

This is one of my favorite scenes in the Gospels. (But I have to admit I have many favorites.) Here is a little serving girl from "Hicksville," from up yonder in the hill country – "Can anything good come from Nazareth?" And here she stands in a very sophisticated suburb of the capital city in the midst of her affluent and cultured kin. I am sure she was well aware how far down their long noses they looked to take any notice of this country cousin. Yet with radiant, humble joy she steps to the center and begins to sing:

> My soul proclaims the greatness of the Lord.
> And my spirit exults in God my savior;
> because he has looked upon his lowly handmaid.
> Yes, from this day forward all generations will
> call me blessed, [Oh, how I would love to have
> seen the faces of her high-class, priestly kin at
> that moment: Who does she think she is!] for the
> Almighty has done great things for me.
> Holy is his name.

And she went on to sing: "His mercy reaches from age to age for those who fear him." Yes, even to you and me. If we are worthy, like Mary, to hear Elizabeth's "Blessed are you who believed that the promise made by the Lord would be fulfilled," then we, too, will see His power active in our lives. And like Mary our proper response is no falsely modest disclaimer, but a proud, humble boast: "My soul proclaims the greatness of the Lord . . . He has looked upon his lowly servant . . . the Almighty has done great things for me. Holy is his name." Praise, glorification, thanksgiving – that is the mark of the faithfull Christian. "I thank you for the wonder of my being." "Filled with joy by the Holy Spirit, Jesus said, 'I thank you, Father, Lord of heaven and earth, for you hide these things from the learned and the clever but you reveal them to the little ones.'"

"WHY HAVE YOU DONE THIS . . ."

As the wonder of God's life in us and the working of His power through us become a settled fact in our lives, we can, in spite of the wonder, begin to take it for granted. "God is with me. Things should be as they are. After all God is God, and he loves me. So it is."

I have been strongly struck by the words of the Gospel: "They [Mary and Joseph] *assumed* he was with them." All the more the shock then when suddenly the awful truth strikes home: He is not with us. Then the pain, the agony, the fear, the self-questioning. The fumbling through the dark may last more than three days and nights. But if we persevere in the seeking we will at last come to such a perception of His presence that we can cry out, "Why have you done this . . ."

This seemingly strange pericope of Jesus' escapade as a twelve-year-old has something very important to teach us. And as we struggle with the experience it illumines, it is good to know that Mary has been through it, too, in her own way and so can understand and show us the way. We think and feel we are moving along just as the Lord wills. He is close. Life is peaceful and full. Then one day in the midst of our regularly scheduled events we suddenly become aware of a terrible change. He seems to have dropped out of sight. The classical authors speak of dark nights of sense and spirit. Little consolation! We can only perceive: He is not here. Like Mary we must perseveringly search. We must continue our prayer in faith. We must search the Scriptures. And we should not be surprised if our spirit cries out like Mary to its God: "Why have You done this to me?" Finally, as the darkness begins to clear – for at first even this is seemingly impossible – we have to hear in faith the response that Mary heard: "Did you not know I must be about my Father's business?" Yes, He is about His Father's business of deepening and purifying our faith and love. And we must continue on, seeking in the dark, never doubting His love, believing that the darksome search of centering prayer, of Sacred Scripture, of the daily task is what is called for from us as our part in the accomplishment of His Father's business. "For I have come down from heaven, not to do my own will, but the will of him who sent me: and this is the will of him who sent me, that I should lose nothing of all that he has given me, but raise it up on the last day."

Mary, too, had to take this on faith. "She did not understand what he meant." But the trial was soon over: "He went down with them." And she "stored up all this in her heart," learning, preparing for the greater trials ahead, till that bleak Saturday, which has made every Saturday hers, when the whole of the faith of the Church was stored in that heart and the whole of creation awaited an Easter dawn.

"THEY HAVE NO WINE"

But let us turn to a happier scene, where faith is luminous and Christ is in our midst and we are in the midst of great joy. Here Mary teaches us how to pray. To put her lesson in a word: no need is too human or trivial, just simply set it before the Lord for He loves.

This is another of my favorite scenes. One might ask whatever possessed Mary to go to Christ with this particular need. I can feel for our Lord and well understand His seemingly enigmatic answer that has kept the Scripture scholars busy. Things were not transpiring exactly as He might have planned. "After all, Mother, do you want it to go down in history that the first sign the Son of God worked on his saving mission was to turn out more booze for the boys after they had drunk the house dry?" No, it was not the way one would have expected the script to be written. But Mary had expressed a need – the need of others which she had made her own – and her faith in His love never wavered. "I tell you solemnly, if you have faith and do not waver in your heart, not only will you do what I have done, but even greater things . . . If you have faith, everything you ask for in prayer you will receive."

In prayer we do not need to articulate our own needs repeatedly, nor the multitudinous needs of our sisters and brothers. No, we need simply to identify with them and then stand before the Lord in the prayer of unwavering faith, the prayer of being and presence, a centering prayer, and He will see and grant all our needs. "Your heavenly Father knows you need all these things. So set your heart on the kingdom . . . and all these will be given you as well."

"DO WHATEVER HE TELLS YOU"

Mary's final word is simple and straightforward. It sums everything up: "Do *whatever* he tells you." This is the practical response of faith. "He is my God, He is my Lord, He is my love. He knows what is best." He does, indeed, at times seem to draw straight with crooked lines. But "for those who love God, *all things* work together unto good."

Yes, I suppose we do have to say that the Scriptures tell us relatively little of Mary. But will you not agree that what they do tell us gives us more than enough to work with? There are many unaccounted-for hours, days, weeks, months, and years in the life of the Virgin. Or are there? Does not Saint Luke sum them all up for us: "As for Mary, she treasured all these things and pondered them in her heart."

From the moment of her conceiving she must have begun to center within with a new liveliness.

And as that Child came forth and she worshiped the One who was at her center in Him, new depths of the mystery of our oneness in God in Christ must have unfolded for her. So when her Son spoke to her on Calvary she fully understood.

Mary's last word to us is, "Do whatever he tells you." As we search the Scriptures we find only one occasion when He tells her to do something. And we can be very sure she does it with all her heart. When Christ looked down from the Cross He gave her a simple but heart-rending command that would keep her busy till the end of time: "Woman, behold your son." And Mary, who had dwelt at the center and knew the unity of the human family, as she turned to John and embraced him, took in her arms and to her heart every man and woman who would ever live, each one of us. And ever since then she has taken the needs of each as her own and with unperturbable faith she says to her Son: "They have no . . ."

With such being the reality, with Mary as model and mother, who cannot confidently set forth to live a life of practical faith?

A Rule of Life

AS I SIT IN THE CONFERENCE ROOM IN OUR RETREAT house, my view reaches out across the fields to the woods north of the abbey. In the wintertime, at the beginning of a retreat, my thoughts often go back to an experience I had in those woods about twenty years ago. At that time Father Richard and I were working together on our farm. Father Richard came from a Minnesota farm and is a really hard worker. During the summer our hours were long. I expected, when winter came, we would get a chance to "put our feet up." But as winter set in, Father found one job after the other to keep us busy. Finally, we had our first heavy snowfall, and it lay deep on the land. I thought, "At last I'll get a day off." But when work time came, Father Richard announced it would be a good day to mark out a trail through the north woods on which to move our heavy machinery in the spring. As we trudged out across the field, knee-deep and sometimes waist-deep in snow, I wasn't the happiest of monks. We plunged into the woods and started marking trees to route the future trail. But soon we couldn't find the woods for the trees. After ducking around thickets, skirting gullies, pushing through brush, we were not sure which way was north. The leaden sky offered no sun to guide us. At this point I said to Father Richard rather facetiously, "Why don't you just shinny up that nice high tree there and shout out directions and I'll mark the trees?" To my amazement – and chagrin – Father Richard proceeded to do just what I had suggested, and soon was at the top of the tree, shouting down directions. And thus we proceeded, Richard going up the highest tree he could find and I moving along on the ground at his direction. Before the afternoon was out, we had gotten through the woods. The trail we marked is there till this day.

It seems to me that life is like that journey through the woods. As we move along, day by day, meeting the daily demands, following the attractions of the moment, going this way and that, we can easily miss the woods for the trees. We need to shinny up a high tree and see where we are going. Perhaps we will find ourselves out on a limb, a bit off course, headed down a dead end. A time of retreat offers an opportunity for going up a high tree. Besides our annual period of renewal and refreshment – one can go fairly far off route in the course of a year – we can certainly use at least a monthly retreat day for such a "climb."

But it will do us little good to get up on top of a high tree to take a look if we have no idea where we are heading. Happiness consists in knowing what we want, and in knowing we have it or are on the way to getting it. Most of us experience unhappiness because we do not know what we want or refuse to make a choice. Also, we sometimes set our hearts on the impossible, like a child crying for the moon, or want what is not really good for us or truly responsive to our needs.

We do have freedom. It is one of the most precious things that God has given to the human person. And we need to use it to choose our goal. But there are definite perimeters to our realistic options. We have to consult our nature as man or woman, with its needs and potencies. The baptized has a new nature, a Christ-nature, having been made a partaker of Christ. And its exigencies must also be respected. In addition there are our gifts and talents, charism and vocation. All of these must be recognized and respected in choosing our goal and the means of getting there. But within the context of all these there is still room for free discrimination. Sometimes very difficult choices must be made. The choice to cultivate one gift may mean having to neglect others. It is the trauma of facing many options and having to give up many very good and attractive possibilities in order to pursue fruitfully a chosen one or two which sometimes paralyzes, leaving one to drift through life, taking what comes, and missing out on real happiness.

The key to happiness and success in life is a choice of ultimate and immediate goals that are realistic and truly satisfying, a clear grasp of effective means for attaining them and a realistic use of their means. To further this we have found a simple but perhaps demanding exercise quite helpful.

First of all we take some time to come into the presence of God and to seek the help and guidance of the Holy Spirit. It is good to read something like 1 Corinthians 2, which we have cited in the Foreword, to help us realize how completely dependent we are on Him in the discernment of questions that

vitally affect our life and happiness as persons who
have been baptized into Christ and share in His
divine life and nature.

We then take four sheets of paper.

On the *first* we seek to express as precisely and
concisely as possible *our goals in life,* what we want
to do with our lives, what we want to get out of life
and put into it. This should be very realistic, listening
deeply to our nature as man or woman, our Christ-
nature, our vocation or charism, our gifts and talents. Satisfactorily responding to these, we have then
to make what choices are necessary to concretize the
goals of our journey so that we have something on
which we can really set our sights.

On the *second sheet* of paper we seek to list as
concisely yet completely as possible *all that we need
to do or acquire in order to attain our determined goals.*
We should be very concrete here, and practical. We
should include the basic needs of our nature, such as
sleep, food, friendship, work, study, etc.; the needs
of our Christ-nature, such as that amount of prayer,
sacred reading, etc., that we need to be satisfactorily
responding to the Father; and then those things necessary to fulfill our vocation and all the other
choices we have made.

As we come to the *third sheet,* we should prayerfully look back over a significant period of time, a
few months to a year or so. Perhaps this could be the
time since our last retreat, or since our life took a
significant turn through graduation or a new job or
something of that sort. Looking at this period we
should try to perceive and note *all the things in our
life:* situations, events, activities, our own passions

or emotions, etc., *which have been hindering us from attaining our goals.*

Finally, on the *fourth sheet* – and this might be the most difficult part of the exercise – we should try to formulate for ourselves a *rule or program of life,* on a daily, weekly, and monthly cycle. With this we seek to assure that there is place in our life for all those things we need to do to attain our goals and to eliminate those things we experienced as obstacles. Important in this is a monthly retreat day, or some other regular periodical "climbing up a high tree" to see where we are. This is important not only to see if we are actually following our rule of life. It is important so that we may experience, in a very conscious way, that happiness that comes from knowing we are actually moving along toward the attainment of our goals.

Some may experience a negative reaction at the thought of seeking to impose on themselves a rule of life. This may arise from past experiences with rules that constricted life instead of supporting it, or one's perception of rules as doing this. But a rule of life is not meant to be a symmetrical trellis that forces the vital movements of life to conform to some artificial pattern. Life should be a luxuriant vine, engrafted deeply into the Vine that is Christ, and sending shoots out in all directions to draw in, as fully as possible, nourishing experiences of reality. The trellis of the rule is there to support the vine, to guide its growth in the most fruitful of directions; never to constrict or truncate any of life's vitality.

Life does tend to go in many directions, reaching for many goals, being affected by innumerable influences each and every day. In this vital context, a rule is not so much a thing to be lived, but rather a norm to measure ourselves against, to assure that none of the things we have perceived as necessary for the attainment of our goals (sheet two) are in fact being neglected.

With an instrument such as this in our possession we can hope to move along more successfully and satisfyingly. Undoubtedly we will have to update our rule periodically. In my experience almost every retreat day, as I review my personal rule of life, I find that it is advisable to revise it in one respect or another to respond to the evolution that has been taking place in my life and situation. In this way it remains a life-supporting instrument.

As a recent workshop was drawing to a close, one of the priests voiced a fear. A number of times previously in his life, in the course of a retreat or workshop, he had had, just as at this workshop, a Taboric experience. Then he returned to the plain of everyday service, and soon, in spite of all resolutions, the light faded. He feared, in spite of the wonder of this new opening into the realm of contemplative union with God, the light might again fade. If the reader has entered into the experiences shared in these pages, she or he might at this point know something of the Father's fear. The simple proposal made in this Epilogue is a response to this. If we do something very concrete and practical to support our daily fidelity to dialogical reading and centering prayer, the light of Tabor will not fade. But, like Peter, even after many years, we will be able to proclaim steadfastly, because of our own daily experience, the power of Christ, the Father's delight, and the presence of the Holy Spirit, "for we were with Him on the Holy Mountain."

All praise to Him!

Select Bibliography

Books

Clark, Thomas, et al., *Finding Grace at the Center* (Petersham, Mass.: St. Bede's Publications).

Keating, Thomas, *Invitation to Love: The Way of Christian Contemplation* (New York, N.Y.: Continuum).
_____, *Open Mind, Open Heart: The Contemplative Dimension of the Gospel* (New York, N.Y.: Continuum).

Main, John, *Moment of Christ: The Path of Meditation* (London: Darton, Longmans, and Todd).
Merton, Thomas, *Contemplation in a World of Action* (New York, N.Y.: Doubleday).
_____, *The Climate of Monastic Prayer* (Kalamazoo, Mich.: Cistercian Publications).

Pennington, M. Basil, *Call to the Center: The Gospel's Invitation to Deeper Prayer* (Hyde Park, N.Y.: New City Press).
_____, *Centered Living: The Way of Centering Prayer* (New York, N.Y.: Doubleday).
_____, *Centering Prayer: Renewing an Ancient Christian Prayer Form* (New York, N.Y.: Doubleday).

William of Saint Thierry, *On Contemplating God, Prayer, Meditations* (Kalamazoo, Mich.: Cistercian Publications).

Audio Cassettes

Keating, Thomas, *Contemplative Prayer*, 4 cassettes (Butler, N.J.: Contemplative Outreach).

_____, *Diving Therapy*, 2 cassettes (Butler, N.J.: Contemplative Outreach).

_____, *Journey Toward Contemplation*, 4 cassettes (Butler, NJ: Contemplative Outreach).

Pennington, M. Basil, *A Centered Life*, 8 cassettes (Kansas City, Mo.: Credence Cassettes).

_____, *The Contemplative Attitude* (Kansas City, Mo.: Credence Cassettes).

Video Cassettes

Keating, Thomas, *The Spiritual Journey*, 26 cassettes (Butler, N.J.: Contemplative Outreach).

Pennington, M. Basil, *A Matter of Love*, 4 30-minute presentations (Kansas City, Mo.: Credence Cassettes).

_____, *Contemplation for Everyone*, 3 cassettes (Deerfield Beach, Fla.: Food for the Poor).

_____, *Faith: Journey to the Center*, 6 conferences (Kansas City, Mo.: Credence Cassettes).

_____, *How to Center Your Life*, 4 30-minute presentations (Allen, Tex.: RCL Enterprises).

_____, *Opening the Contemplative Dimension* (Kansas City, Mo.: Credence Cassettes).

The Second Vatican Council reminds us that every baptized Christian is called to share in this deep quiet union with our Lord in prayer.